STUDIO PROJECTS IN ART HISTORY

Written & Illustrated
by
William Reid

J. Weston Walch, Publisher
Portland, Maine

1   2   3   4   5   6   7   8   9   10

ISBN 0-8251-1661-9

Copyright © 1990
J. Weston Walch, Publisher
P.O. Box 658 • Portland, Maine 04104-0658

Printed in the United States of America

Contents

PART IV: EARLY MODERN ART (1750–1900) . . . 119

PART V: MODERN ART (TWENTIETH CENTURY)... 153

Foreword

Years ago, concluding a year traveling in Europe, I worked my way to northern Spain. The money I had earned as a printer's assistant in Germany was nearing an end, as was my wander year. One place I still wanted to visit was one or more of the prehistoric caves of northern Spain. Outside the village of Santillana I joined a few other tourists being led through the cave of Altamira, described by some as the Sistine Chapel of prehistoric art.

The caretaker of the cave, understanding that I was a student, allowed me to remain alone in the cave after the tour was finished. Lying on the floor looking up at the ceiling paintings of Altamira, I stared and thought, as students do. There I remained for a quarter of an hour.

That was too long ago and I realize, now that Altamira has been closed to the public, that I know those paintings more from book reproductions than from anything I saw that day. What remains is the thrill of having looked upon the art some person painted 14,000 years ago. That someone touched me with his feel for color, sense of line, and creative spirit. Ever since those moments alone in Altamira I have taken every opportunity to demonstrate to others how art, more than any other experience, is capable of placing us closer to peoples of the past. Time is wiped out, and the joy of line, color, and visual concept can travel 14,000 years in an instant.

Once, in northern France, I took a *pension* room one block from the great Gothic cathedral of Amiens. I stayed there for a week. There is not much to do in Amiens; most visitors sweep through to see the cathedral and then move on, seldom staying the night. But I was determined to live by and with that building for a week. I attended its services, sat alone in the great nave, examined its facade sculpture, ate sandwiches beneath its flying buttresses, and walked by it at night when floodlights lit its towers. I got what I was looking for: a sense of the spiritual nature which had built the cathedral and sustained it for some seven centuries. Art — both the cathedral itself and its supporting art — had shown it to me.

Once again art had put me in touch with persons of the distant past and made my own experience fuller by giving me something of theirs. Whenever I am able to show art's potential for bridging time, I leap at the chance. Here I go again.

Introduction

Doing something with one's hands is a learning process. Every artist mentioned in this book learned by doing: by drawing, painting, carving, making. Learning by doing is the underlying precept of this book, one that has already appeared in several Walch craft books. This time students learn by making art in the way the great works in museums were created.

This book adapts a variety of art techniques and styles to classroom projects. There is no intent to make students into Op artists or Baroque still-life painters. Nor is it imagined that anyone will become a Matisse, Rembrandt, or Polyclitus by practicing the projects of this book. However, by imitating techniques and styles from various historical periods, students gain insight into artistic thought and a better understanding of art history.

Each project in this book has a learning goal: to demonstrate some concept in the history of Western art. For example, there is a number of color exercises. They may seem to be simple "color the picture" games, but they go further. They give experience in selecting and arranging colors. They demonstrate different approaches to color composition. They show the color thinking behind various art styles.

Painting has dominated Western art from the Renaissance to today. Projects devoted to the Renaissance and subsequent periods cannot teach painting, but they can illuminate the many styles and approaches to painting since the fifteenth century.

Like most art-history books, this one takes a chronological look at Western art. Because the projects examine various phases of art, they are useful for many class projects not related to art history. At the back of the book there is an index which groups the projects according to subject: design, composition, technique, color, and so on.

These projects are intended for supplementary study. Color reproductions from other art-history books, slides, and museum visits support the aim of the book. The book's illustrations are not reproductions of the works of art in question. Instead, they are line copies of the appropriate works of art. This technique is used for two reasons: One, line drawings reproduce more clearly as photocopies than do photographs; two, in most cases specific points are being made about the work of art, and the drawn copy picks out the significant detail and clarifies it visually. A table at the end of the book indicates the site of the original work from which each drawing has been taken.

How the Book Works

The book is divided into thirty chapters, each devoted to a particular period or style of Western art. Each chapter begins with a teacher introduction. This page includes an overview of the period, suggestions for giving students a feeling for the period, and a list of significant works or artists of the period. From the Renaissance on, the list is confined to painters.

The rest of each chapter consists of reproducible pages, that is, pages which can be photocopied and handed out to students for information or work.

The first reproducible page of each chapter gives a general description of the period or style. It includes the dates during which the period or style was important, even though it might have begun earlier and lingered for years later. Dates for the twentieth century mark the point at which a movement first made a noticeable impression on the public. A small map helps locate the principal regions or countries where the style developed.

Following this reproducible introduction to the period or movement are several project pages. Most projects are confined to a single page. The project is explained on the page and, in most cases, work is completed on the reproduced sheet. However, the project may be completed on larger drawing paper or other material. Each reproducible page can be photocopied and handed out for students to work on their own. Or, any project can be expanded upon and given orally as a class project without reproducing the book page.

This is a resource book. It may be used in a variety of ways — to supplement art-class study or cultural-period study, or simply as a source of art projects or exercises. Because the projects can be tied to famous works of art, they have several dimensions. If they help students to understand and enjoy historical art, then the aim of the book has been realized.

PART I:

ANCIENT ART

CHAPTER 1

Prehistoric Art

The art of Stone and Bronze Age cultures can be described as prehistoric. Some of this art has survived into the twentieth century. The oldest has been found in Czechoslovakia, where carbon-14 dating has revealed the age of two ivory heads to be 26,000 years old. Their original purpose remains a mystery, although their facial features are distinct and individual enough to suggest they may have been intended as portraits.

Better known because of their frequent reproduction are the cave paintings of certain caves in northern Spain, the Pyrenees, and the Dordogne region of France. Given their site — the rough walls of dark cave interiors — the paintings are as remarkable for their quality as they are for their age of 14,000 years.

There is an air of mystery about prehistoric art. Thanks to modern research methods, we know who created the art, when, and how, but just why it was produced has never been satisfactorily determined. Usually a vague religious reason is put forward as a theory, but no definitive answers exist.

In presenting this art to students, let this air of mystery linger. An unsolved mystery stimulates curiosity. Let the students try to grasp the sensation of looking at art carved 26,000 years ago or painted 14,000 years ago. Through art they come in direct contact with people who lived tens of thousands of years in the past.

This chapter's painting project describes mixing earth powders with animal fat or honey, which analysis has shown to be the medium of cave-painting pigments. More important than the final product is the experience of handling such primitive, natural materials. The carving project is not done with ivory, of course, but with soap, which is easily carved and can simulate ivory in appearance.

Significant art dates:

Czechoslovakian ivory heads, c. 24,000 B.C.
Cave paintings of Lascaux, France, 15,000–12,000 B.C.
Cave paintings of Altamira, Spain, 15,000–12,000 B.C.

Prehistoric Art
24,000 and 12,000 B.C.

Can you imagine a time 26,000 years ago? That long ago someone carved this head in a piece of ivory. For tens of thousands of years it lay buried until it was finally unearthed in modern Czechoslovakia. When you look at it you can imagine some prehistoric artist carving the ivory chunk, chipping away pieces with a stone knife, smoothing edges with a stone file. You have come into direct contact with that very ancient person through art.

Major prehistoric European sites

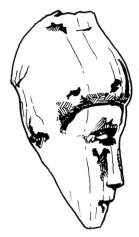

Ivory carving

About 14,000 years ago artists painted pictures in caves in France and Spain. Because they lived by hunting, their subjects were usually animals. Sometimes they painted arrows or spears in the sides of the animals, as if "killing" them in a painting would help them to kill during a hunt. These people lived in the mouths of caves, but painted their pictures deep within their caverns. There, beneath the light of torches, the artists decorated the rough walls for prehistoric religious celebrations. If we know nothing more about the purpose of these ancient paintings, their artists have communicated to us their understanding of their animal subjects and a sense of beauty which impresses us 140 centuries later.

Cave Painting

Project 1: Carved Head

This page illustrates one of the ivory heads carved in Czechoslovakia 26,000 years ago. It is a remarkable demonstration of how early in human history art began. You can carve a similar head, but in soap, not ivory. Soap is easy to carve and, if white or tan in color, has the appearance of ivory. Using a hobby knife for carving, copy this head or create one of your own.

1. Draw the front of the head on the soap.
2. Cut away pieces to make the general shape of the front.
3. Draw the profile of the head on the side.
4. Cut away pieces to shape the profile.
5. Draw the details of the face on the front.
6. With the basic shape now cut, carve the details of the face.
7. When the carving is complete, rough corners can be smoothed with a damp cloth.

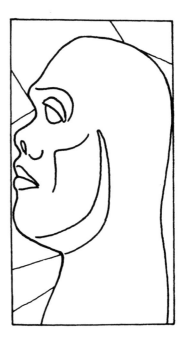

Project 2: Prehistoric Painting

This illustration copies a picture someone painted on a cave wall in France some 14,000 years ago. You can create a similar picture with the materials prehistoric artists used. Their paint consisted of powdered earth materials mixed with fat, honey, or blood. Therefore, their colors were confined to reds, oranges, browns, and yellows. For black they used burnt charcoal and for white they used ash.

1. Make earth-pigment powders by filing the edges of bricks and unglazed tile pieces with a fine metal file.

2. Collect melted cooking fat in a clean can or use honey for mixing your powdered pigments.

3. Paint on a flat stone, first cleaned with cleansing powder.

4. Draw the outline of your animal picture with a stick of artist's charcoal or charcoal pencil.

5. Put the separate piles of powdered color in a pie plate. Soften the animal fat, but do not melt, or dip out a saucer of honey. Using a watercolor brush, dip into the softened fat or honey and mix with one of the color powders.

6. Use this paint to color within the design outline.

7. When finished, clean your brush well with hand soap.

Kept at room temperature and not the chilly interior of a cave, the fat pigment will remain oily, the honey pigment sticky, and both can rub away. Therefore, handle the finished cave picture with care.

CHAPTER 2

Mesopotamian Art

Nineveh, Babylon, Ur of the Chaldees, Jericho — these are all names with a familiar ring, great cities mentioned in the Old Testament. They are also great cities of art, for each of them has been located and excavated, giving up works of art to the archaeologist's spade while adding validity to Biblical accounts. These cities were part of Mesopotamia, a region now occupied by modern Iraq and parts of Turkey and Iran. However, Mesopotamia influenced cultures beyond those borders.

Excavations at Çatal Hüyük in Turkey have revealed a flourishing urban culture as early as 7000 B.C. Later came the Sumerian civilization, which lasted from about 3000 B.C. to 2000 B.C., the first period of Babylon from 1900 to 1600 B.C., the Assyrian domination from 900 to 600 B.C., the Neo-Babylonian kingdom with the familiar name of Nebuchadnezzar from 612 to 538 B.C., and finally the Persian Empire from 538 B.C. to the coming of Alexander the Great in 331 B.C.

Although the arts of these cultures differ, there are similarities. For instance, the gods and guardians of their state religions resemble each other. These mythical beings inspire Project 3 in this chapter, letting students create their own part-human, part-animal creatures. Common objects used in Mesopotamian cultures were seal stones, or hard clay cylinders with incised pictures and writing. When rolled across soft clay they left an imprint for state accounting and identifying ownership of market goods. The third project of this chapter is inspired from several examples of early Sumerian shell inlay, adapted to a simpler student method.

Tying this period to familiar Biblical accounts gives added meaning; for example, the golden calf worshipped by the Israelites during the Exodus is a clear connection with the use of gold and precious materials and the worship of animal gods by the Mesopotamian neighbors. Daniel in the Lion's den may simply have been a symbolic way of describing the prophet's confinement in Babylon, for the city's gate and walls were covered in tiles depicting wild animals. The Tower of Babel was probably a Mesopotamian ziggurat with a pagan temple on top. At first Mesopotamian art seems far removed from us in time and place, but it can be brought close by a simple Sunday School lesson.

Significant art dates:

Standard of Ur, c. 2700 B.C.	Ishtar Gate of Babylon, c. 575 B.C.
Stele of Hammurabi, c. 1760 B.C.	Reliefs of Persepolis, c. 500 B.C.
Ashurbanipal Hunting Lions, c. 650 B.C.	

Mesopotamian Art
6000 B.C.–323 B.C.

Civilized societies first appeared in Mesopotamia, the region now occupied by Iran and parts of Iraq and Turkey. Catal Hüyük, in what has become Turkey, was already a flourishing culture by 7000 B.C. For thousands of years wars raged across Mesopotamia as great cities rose and fell. The names of some of them — Ur, Nineveh, and Babylon — are mentioned in the Old Testament accounts of the Bible, as are the names of the various peoples of Mesopotamia: the Sumerians, the Babylonians, the Assyrians, the Hittites, and the Persians.

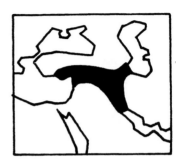

**Mesopotamia in
the Middle East**

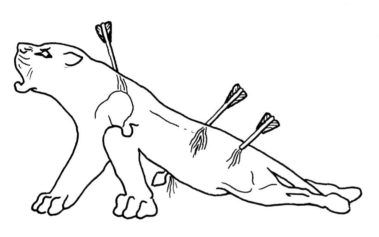

Assyrian animal carving

All of these people produced art similar in spirit and subject matter. It frequently included animal subjects, for they hunted some wild animals and domesticated others. They often depicted their kings hunting bulls and lions as demonstration of their power over neighboring enemies. This dying lioness was carved by an Assyrian artist about 650 B.C.

Mesopotamian builders raised temples on the tops of high, artificial mounds climbed by ramps and stairs. These mounds are called *ziggurats,* and their ruins remain today. The Biblical Tower of Babel and Hanging Gardens of Babylon were probably ziggurats.

The walls of Mesopotamian cities were decorated with carvings and tiles illustrating animal subjects. Such grand cities and the objects of gold, silver, and precious stones found in their ruins indicate that the people of Mesopotamia enjoyed a rich, if not always peaceful, life.

Project 3: Mesopotamian Monsters

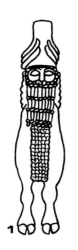

Monsters haunted ancient religions as gods and guardian figures. In Mesopotamia those monsters were usually part human and part beast. Here is a selection of monsters found in Mesopotamian art. On the back of this sheet, use the same formula of part animal or bird and part person to create a modern monster to dwell in the dark alleys of your town.

1. Guardian, man-headed bull
2. Eagle-headed winged genie
3. Dagon, god of farming

4. Marduc, the creator
5. Demon of disease

Project 4: Cylinder Seal

When excavating ancient Mesopotamian cities, archaeologists have found many cylinder seals. These seals have small pictures and letters cut into them. The two illustrated are slightly larger than their actual size. The one on the left was made about 2300 B.C., its letters identifying the owner. The one on the right was made before 3000 B.C. Such seals were rolled across clay, leaving an impression of the carving as a record of ownership of goods or as an official's seal on some document written in clay. Generally cut from stone, some seals were also made of clay, the material which you will use. Make certain it is clay which will dry hard.

1. Plan a design for the seal which includes your name and initials as well as an object, animal, or person in the spirit of Mesopotamian art.

2. Roll out a cylinder of clay approximately ¾″ thick.

3. Cut the ends square so the cylinder is 1½″ long.

4. Cut your design into the damp clay with a small-bladed hobby knife.

5. When the cylinder has dried hard, use it by rolling across softened wax, impressing your design into the material.

Project 5: Sumerian Shell Inlay

Any inlay is made by fitting pieces for a design into a background material. This sheet illustrates a detail of pieces of shell inlay, in the shape of soldiers, laid into lapis lazuli, a dark blue stone popular with artists in ancient Mesopotamia. The original was made about 2700 B.C. in the Sumerian city of Ur. Your inlay will be made of more easily worked materials.

1. Plan an inlay design 2″ by 4″.

2. If you live near the sea or a lake, you could collect shell material. Cut flat pieces to shape with a hobby knife and refine the shape by sanding the edges. If shell is not available, use thin pieces of white plastic.

3. From kitchen foil make a small tray 2″ by 4″ with ⅛″-high sides.

4. Melt wax candles or paraffin tinted with a wax crayon into the foil tray by setting it in a pan over an electric hot plate. Do not melt over an open flame.

5. When the wax has melted, remove from heat. While still soft, press the shell or plastic pieces into the wax, following your design plan. The example illustrated here is based on another Sumerian shell inlay.

6. Let the wax harden, then display with the foil left as backing.

CHAPTER 3

Egyptian Art

Until recent archaeological discoveries revealed certain sites in the Middle East to be older, the Eyptian civilization was considered the world's oldest. However, this conclusion does not detract from the importance of ancient Egyptian art. The great pyramids stand as the single survivors of the seven wonders of the ancient world, and two centuries of digging in Egypt have unearthed great treasures to be deposited in major art museums.

Its 3,000 years of consistent art styles is remarkable to think of. It is a time span which, in looking backward from the present day, carries us to a period before the rise of classical Greece. If it is difficult for us and our students to comprehend this great time scale, we can still enjoy the spirit of Egyptian art.

It was a conservative art style supporting kings and priests. Any deviation from the formula stylization was condemned religiously and politically by this highly regulated society. Resisting invasion until being conquered by Alexander the Great in 332 B.C., ancient Egypt's rulers could put a political and religious padlock on their subjects and discourage any artistic change.

To recognize the conservatism of this consistent style is the first step in understanding Egyptian art. Therefore, two of the projects in this chapter concern themselves with stylization. The third deals with a mystery of Egyptian art, hieroglyphics. One project cannot deal with the complex problems of hieroglyphic translation, but it can offer the fun of this secret art code. Hieroglyphic phrases can then be added to the Egyptized art of the other two projects to support student study of this ancient civilization and art.

Significant art dates:

Step Pyramid of Zoser, c. 2750 B.C.
Great Pyramids of Gizeh, c. 2650 B.C.–2575 B.C.
Temple of Queen Hatshepsut, c. 1500 B.C.
Limestone head of Queen Nefertiti, c. 1360 B.C.
Tomb treasures of Tutankhamen, c. 1350 B.C.
Temple of Rameses II, Abu Simbel, 1257 B.C.

Egyptian Art
3000 B.C.–332 B.C.

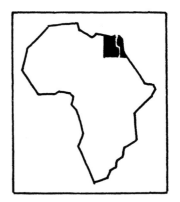

**Egypt in
Northeast Africa**

The Nile, flowing north through Egypt, is the world's longest river. When it enters the country, it passes through dry, rocky Upper Egypt, then into the flatter land of Lower Egypt. Its waters make the land fertile on either side, saving Egypt from being a complete desert. Whenever both Upper and Lower Egypt were united, its ancient civilization prospered. The first time was in 3000 B.C., beginning a 3,000-year civilization.

Nefertiti

This lengthy calendar is divided into ruling dynasties and its periods of power are called kingdoms. During the Old Kingdom (2680–2260 B.C.), ruled by the Third to Sixth Dynasties, the Great Pyramids were built. The Pharaohs of the Middle Kingdom (2130–1790 B.C.), ruled by the Eleventh and Twelfth Dynasties, concentrated on building temples rather than pyramids. So too did the rulers of the New Kingdom (1570–1085 B.C.), the Eighteenth to Twentieth Dynasties. From the New Kingdom also came the carved head of Queen Nefertiti (shown here), the treasures of the tomb of Tutankhamen (King Tut), and the huge statues of Rameses II at Abu Simbel.

Through all its centuries, Egyptian artists worked in a formal, stylized manner, only rarely loosening up to produce more natural-appearing forms. The long, strict rule of the powerful Pharaohs and the severity of the desert environment (saved only by the Nile) encouraged this conservative approach to art.

Studio Projects in Art History

Project 6: Egyptian Figure Proportions

Egyptian artists rendered the human figure in an unusual but logical manner, showing the most interesting angles: the profile of the face and legs, and the front of the torso and eye. They made the figures tall, slim, and wide-shouldered, following strict proportions. It was as if they fitted each figure into a grid, as shown here, always placing the knee on the sixth line from the bottom, the shoulders four from the top and six squares wide, and so on. With the small grid as a guide, draw the figure in the larger grid.

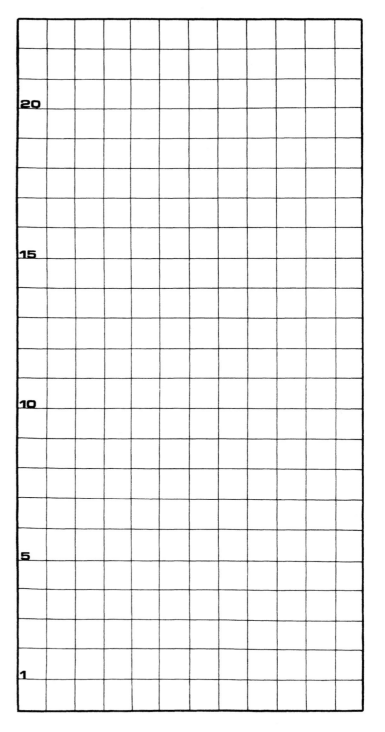

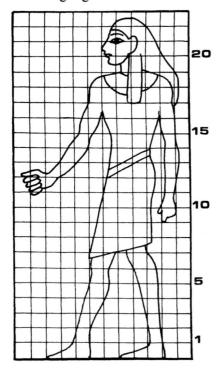

Student Name _____   Date _____

Project 7: Egyptian Temple Columns

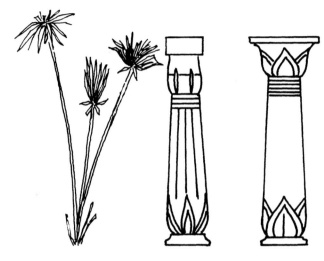

Egyptian temples were mysterious places, dark and mystical, with ceilings held up by thick columns standing as closely as the trees of a forest. The two most common column styles of Egyptian architecture were based on the bud and the open-leafed parts of the papyrus plant, the symbol of Lower Egypt. Like everything in Egyptian art, these column forms were highly stylized. That is, the shape of the plant was considerably changed into a formal design for the column.

Here you see a drawing of a papyrus plant and the two styles of columns inspired by it, one resembling a bundle of budding plant stalks and the other the open leaves. In the left frame, sketch a common plant of your area. Then design a stylized representation of the plant in the frame next to it.

15   *Studio Projects in Art History*

Project 8: Egyptian Hieroglyphs

Egyptian painting and sculpture often include writing called hieroglyphs. These are tiny picture symbols which represent either the object pictured or certain letter sounds. These sounds are always consonants, so the vowel sounds must be guessed at. If the hieroglyph has a vertical line beneath, the word is the object pictured. If there are three vertical lines, the word is the plural of the object. If there are no lines, it represents a particular consonant sound.

Study the line of eye hieroglyphs below. The first has a single line and stands for the word *eye*. The second has three lines, so the word is *eyes*. The third and fourth have no lines, so the symbol represents the sound of the letters *YR*. If you add the vowel sound *ou* to it, the hieroglyph could be read as *your*. Add *ea* and it could represent the word *year*.

Can you write a phrase here using hieroglyphs from the table below?

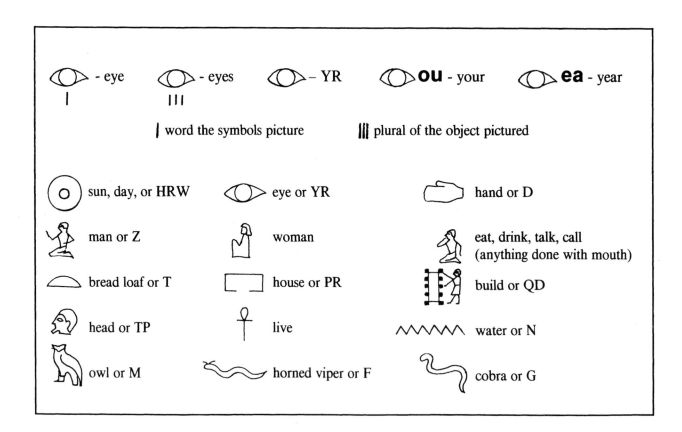

CHAPTER 4

Aegean Art

When Heinrich Schliemann began digging for mythical Troy on the shores of the Aegean, he opened a new chapter in art history. His excavations in Turkey, and later in Greece, at Mycenae and elsewhere, uncovered an art of the past that was until that time unknown. Named for the principal site, it became known as Mycenaean or Helladic art. Several decades later, Arthur Evans unearthed an even more ancient site at mythical Knossos on Crete, revealing art works similar to the Mycenaean, although older, and called Minoan art. Together they make up ancient Aegean art.

The initial excitement over these finds hung on the historical validity they gave to ancient Greek myths, offering new insights into interpretations of ancient history. One project of this chapter demonstrates the truth of one of Homer's statements in the *Iliad,* that Mycenae was rich in gold. Historical validity also figures in the Minoan bull fresco, the other project, for the Minotaur of mythology was part bull. The faces that students will copy in gold foil are now treasures of the Mycenaean gallery in the National Archaeological Museum of Athens.

Beyond adding credence to myths, Aegean art stands on its own. The flowing lines of Minoan art have the grace and decorative elegance of Art Nouveau. This can be seen in the leaping bull of our Minoan project. Picturing only the fragments unearthed by Evans's crew, students are asked to complete the picture as museum restorers have. Let them use their visual sense and imagination and then compare their product with this illustration, which copies the actual reconstruction in the Archaeology Museum in Iraklion (Candia), Crete. Any knowledge which students have of the epics of Homer can be brought to bear upon their enjoyment of Aegean art.

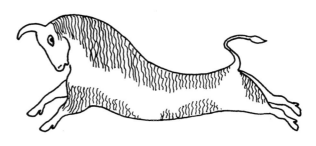

Significant art dates:

Palace at Knossos, c. 1600–1400 B.C.
Toreador fresco, Minoan, c. 1500 B.C.
Harvester vase, Minoan, c. 1500 B.C.
Funeral masks, Mycenaean, c. 1500 B.C.

Vaphio cups, Mycenaean, c. 1500 B.C.
Lion Gate of Mycenae, c. 1300 B.C.
Warrior vase, Mycenaean, c. 1200 B.C.

Aegean Art
2200 B.C.–1200 B.C.

**Mycenae and Crete
in Southeast Europe**

The Aegean Sea lies in the eastern Mediterranean between Greece and Turkey. You may know it as the site of many of the myths of ancient Greece, the wanderings of Odysseus (Ulysses) and the Battle of Troy. For centuries people believed these ancient myths were fairy tales — exciting but untrue stories. Then, one hundred years ago, archaeologists began digging in these mythical places and discovered that people had once lived in them and left art which often fits into the ancient stories.

For example, they discovered on the Greek island of Crete a large palace with many corridors, which could have been the labyrinth of the Minotaur "monster" of myth. And they found many gold objects in the excavations of Mycenae in Greece, a site which the ancient stories described as being "rich in gold."

**Mycenaean
vase figure**

The finds on Crete came from the Minoan civilization, which thrived from about 2000 to 1400 B.C. That was followed by the Mycenaean civilization, also called Helladic, which produced great art from 1500 to 1200 B.C. on the Greek mainland. Mythology tells us that the leader of the Greek army at the Battle of Troy was Agamemnon, the king of Mycenae. Was the soldier pictured here, copied from a Mycenaean vase, one of those who sailed to fight at Troy? Such Aegean art has brought to life the stories of Homer and the mythology of ancient Greece.

Project 9: Minoan Bull Fresco

The art objects which archaeologists discover are not always complete, but only fragments of the original. They then have to imagine how the completed piece might have looked. On this sheet is a drawing of fragments from a wall painting of a bull made about 1500 B.C. and found in an excavated Minoan palace on Crete. King Minos kept bulls for a kind of Minoan bullfight. Because the word for bull in Greek is *tauros,* this was the Minotaur, the monster of the labyrinth of mythology. Using these fragments as your guide, complete the picture of a Minoan bull as museum restorers have actually done.

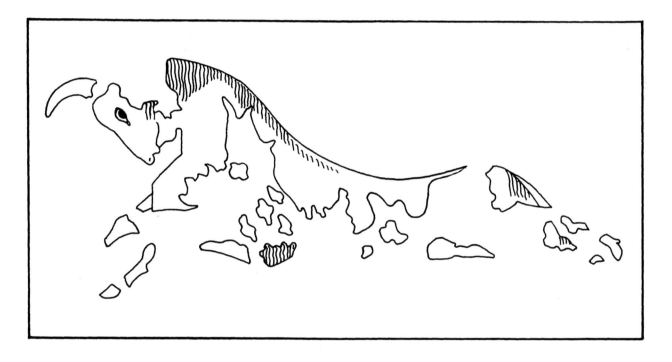

Project 10: Mycenaean Gold Portraits

In *The Iliad* Homer described the ancient city of Mycenae as being rich in gold. Therefore, archaeologists were excited when they found many gold objects at Mycenae, confirming Homer's description. The most dramatic of these finds were full-size death masks shaped in gold sheets—three examples are shown here. You can copy them in gold foil or make similar portrait designs of your own. The originals are life-size, but you can make them smaller.

1. Cut a circle of foil and lay shiny side down on a piece of heavy cloth or sponge rubber.

2. Push your face design into the foil from the back with a blunt instrument, such as the handle end of a paint brush. Also work details from the front.

3. When finished, drip liquid glue into the back. When it hardens, it will support the foil design.

4. To display, glue dark cloth (preferably black) to a piece of stiff cardboard and glue the foil portrait to it.

CHAPTER 5

Greek Art

In centuries past, Greek art and literature were as familiar to students as that of their own day. They learned ancient Greek, read Greek literature, were treated to Greek sculpture (in plaster casts if not originals), and saw Greek architectural ideas in their newest buildings. The twentieth century has changed all that, perhaps correctly so, by creating in the spirit of the present rather than the past. As a result, Greek art has been pushed back with its chronological neighbors, Mesopotamian, Egyptian, and Roman art. There it finds itself in museums, art books, and art-history lectures. Young students come to Greek art with the same unfamiliarity with which they face other ancient arts.

However, Greek art long dominated Western culture for a reason, because it was Classical with a capital "C" to mean a style, and classical with a small "c" to suggest reserve, grace, and refinement. It is no more or less beautiful than a century ago when it was still the basis of artistic taste. Because so much of our culture is based on what was created in Greece 2,500 years ago, Greek art is important for students to explore; but another, perhaps more powerful reason is its beauty and source of enjoyment.

Unlike other ancient arts, Greek art passed through many distinct styles. This chapter limits itself to the late sixth and fifth centuries B.C., when Classical art was being defined. Two projects address sculpture, one of them the all-important matter of Greek proportions and balanced naturalism. The other reveals that Greek marbles were originally colored. An architectural study sheet acknowledges another major Greek art while letting students discover Greek influences in local buildings. The fourth project uses a special kind of Greek vase so students become aware of a minor art which Greek artists made into a major one.

Significant art dates:

Sculptors
　　Phidias, fifth century B.C.
　　Polyclitus, fifth century B.C.
　　Praxiteles, fourth century B.C.
　　Skopas, fourth century B.C.
　　Lysippus, fourth century B.C.

Vase painters
　　Exekias, c. 550–525 B.C.
　　Euphronios, c. 510–500 B.C.

Parthenon architects, c. 448–432 B.C.
　　Iktinos
　　Kallikrates

**Greece in
Southeast Europe**

Greek Art
650 B.C.–146 B.C.

Some 2,500 years ago the people of Greece created art and literature which has inspired the world ever since. Greek philosophers, writers, architects, sculptors, and even pottery painters produced masterpieces.

Greek artists were the first to render the human figure in a natural, relaxed style. Until their time, sculptors had modeled figures to look stiff and formal. You see the difference in the illustrations: the figure on the left, *Standing Youth*, was carved about 600 B.C. It stands erect and stiff, staring straight ahead. Its hair is only decorative ringlets, its muscles more diagrammatic than real. The figure on the right, called *Spear Bearer*, was created 150 years later. In that century and a half, Greek artists had learned to make the human figure appear more relaxed and lifelike.

The style also has a refinement and quiet ease, the same qualities felt in the buildings of the Acropolis in Athens, constructed in the same fifth century B.C. as the *Spear Bearer*. This was the Golden Age of Greece, its art and literature termed *Classical*. The term Classical, with a capital "C," means any art which has been inspired by the art of the Golden Age of Greece, with all its grace and refinement. But most of all, it means the original Classical style of ancient Greece.

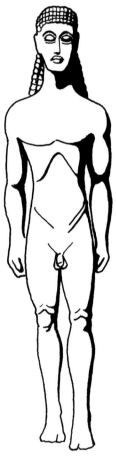

***Standing Youth,*
600 B.C.**

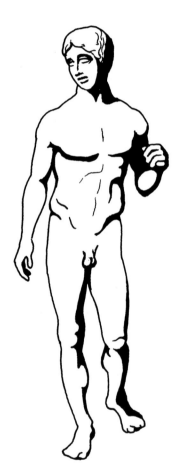

***Spear Bearer,*
c. 450–440 B.C.**

Project 11: Greek Architecture

The architects of ancient Greece designed such beautiful buildings that their styles have influenced architecture ever since. Some buildings you know may have Greek architectural details: for example, banks, churches, other public buildings, and even houses. Each of these Greek details has a particular name. Locate a Greek-style building, note its location below, and check which of these features it has.

building _____

location _____

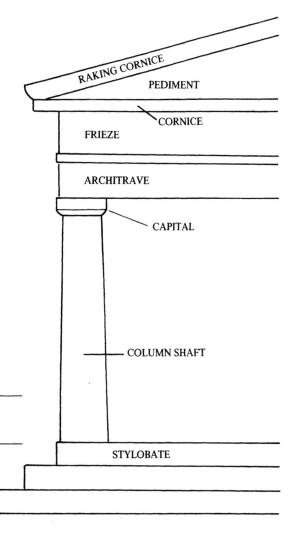

RAKING CORNICE

PEDIMENT

CORNICE

FRIEZE

ARCHITRAVE

CAPITAL

COLUMN SHAFT

STYLOBATE

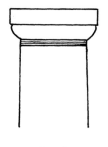

Doric

Ionic

Corinthian

There were three orders (styles) of Greek buildings. The most visible difference is between the capitals of the columns. Try to find these three column capitals in local buildings. Note their location.

Project 12: Color a Kore

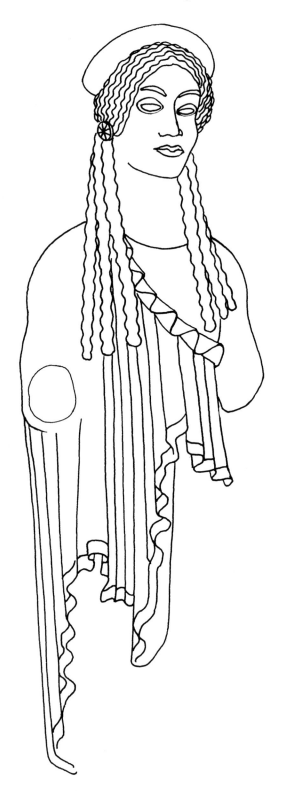

For many years people thought Greek statues had originally been the white of the marble from which they were carved. When statues of young maidens painted in bright colors were found buried on the Acropolis in Athens, people realized that all statues had once been colored. Called *kore,* Greek for "girl," their hair, eyes, brows, and lips were painted. The underblouse and one arm was colored dark, and the borders of the outer garment a contrasting bright color. The flesh and rest of the outer garment were left marble white. Color this drawing of a kore statue, following this color description.

Project 13: Greek Contrapposto Figure

Greek sculptors were the first to give the human figure a natural appearance. Polyclitus (working 450–420 B.C.) used proportions which he felt were ideal for constructing the human figure. His seven-heads-high ideal, shown here on one of his statues called the *Spear Bearer*, is still used today. As did all Greek artists after 450 B.C., he composed the figure in a *contrapposto* posture. A line through the center of the face, chest, and legs makes a shallow S-curve, and all parts slightly oppose one another — one leg relaxed, the other stiff, one shoulder lowered over the raised hip, the head turned opposite to the torso's twist. In the empty diagram frame, construct a figure with Greek proportions and the contrapposto posture.

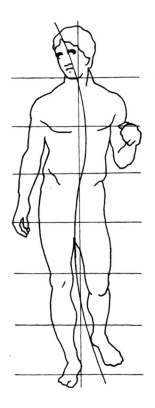

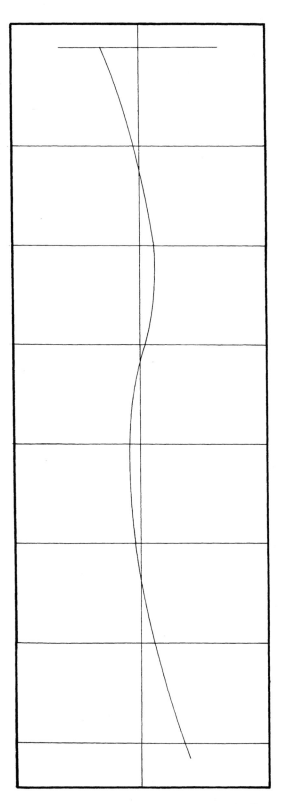

Studio Projects in Art History

Student Name _____ Date _____

Project 14: Athletic Prize Vase

Besides the Olympic Games, ancient Greeks enjoyed other sports contests. Every four years the Athenians celebrated the "Greater Panathenaea," honoring the goddess Athena. Part of the festival included musical, theatrical, and athletic competitions. The athletic trophy was a ceramic vase with a picture of the sport in which the prize was won. The sport figure was always in black with light lined details on an orange-red background. In the empty space of this vase draw a figure for a sport contest in your school.

Studio Projects in Art History

CHAPTER 6

Roman Art

The naturalism of late Greek sculpture suited the Romans when they conquered Greece, shipped its art to Rome, and honored Greek artists as their slaves. They modified the Greek temple to their religious purposes and, rather than using solid marble, built it with a cement and brick core, then veneered it in marble. If this seems to be architecture on the cheap, it was necessary to establish the Roman presence in the far reaches of its vast empire.

The Romans did contribute to the heritage of art. They turned the naturalism they borrowed from Greece into fine portrait sculpture, and elaborated further in the wall frescoes and mosaic floors of their villas and public buildings. The richness of this art survives in the excavated remains of Pompeii and Herculaneum.

Portrait sculpture is represented here with a paraffin-wax carving project, recalling the Roman tradition of making wax portraits of the deceased. Portrait is also the suggested theme of a project inspired by Egyptian art of the Roman era. The paper mosaic project includes two reproducible sheets, providing a choice between a simple and more complicated example.

Cultural periods do not abruptly end. They gradually give way to new ideas. The Roman Empire did not fall in a day. It slowly shifted emphasis and changed face, so it brought to an end the humanistic Classical culture born centuries earlier in Greece, as it ushered in the spiritual culture of the Middle Ages. At the same time it drew the curtain on what we call ancient art.

Significant art dates:

Augustus of Primaporta (statue), 20 B.C.
Ara Pacis altar, 13–9 B.C.
Pompeii wall paintings and buildings, c. 200 B.C.–A.D. 72
Colosseum, A.D. 70–82
Pantheon temple, A.D. 118–125
Equestrian statue of Marcus Aurelius, c. A.D. 165
Arch of Constantine, A.D. 312-315

Roman Art
146 B.C.–A.D. 323

When we think of great empires, ancient Rome comes first to mind. Into the Roman Empire Jesus was born. The Empire included Egypt in Africa, Greece and its colonies, Spain, France, and England. To manage this large territory, the Romans built bridges, roads, and city walls. With talent more for engineering than for art, they turned to conquered Greece for artistic inspiration, copying Greek art and employing Greek artists. Roman buildings are based on Greek architectural ideas, their sculpture on Greek models, and their paintings on Greek themes and styles. Therefore, Roman art and culture is termed *Classical*, like that of Greece.

Roman Empire

Roman portrait sculpture

Roman artists made one major contribution to art: portrait sculpture. The worldly Romans, proud of their accomplishments and themselves, had artists carve marble portraits as realistic-appearing as any modern photograph. This art has left us portraits of Roman aristocrats and rulers, such as that of the Emperor Trajan who reigned from A.D. 98 to 117.

Roman art and remains are found throughout much of western Europe and around the Mediterranean. The most important are at Pompeii and Herculaneum. Both towns were destroyed when Mt. Vesuvius erupted in A.D. 72, destroying and burying them. Modern excavations have unearthed the streets, houses, public buildings, and art of these towns, giving a special insight into ancient Roman art.

Project 15: Roman Wax Portrait

The Romans greatly admired Greek art, of which their art was a late development. However, there was one special kind of Roman art — portrait sculpture. It developed from the tradition of keeping wax masks of deceased relatives in their homes, in the same way we keep photographs of our grandparents and others who have died. Because wax portraits do not last, wealthier Romans had artists carve marble portrait busts. Here is how you can make portrait sculpture from paraffin wax.

1. Draw a portrait, from a model or photograph, both front and profile.
2. Cut a block of paraffin into a square.
3. Use a hobby knife to cut the general shape of the face from the paraffin.
4. Rough-cut the front of the face, using the drawing as a guide.
5. Rough-cut the profile as you develop the face carving.
6. Continue developing the portrait by carving face details.
7. Finish the details and smooth the surface with heated knife blades, screwdrivers, etc.

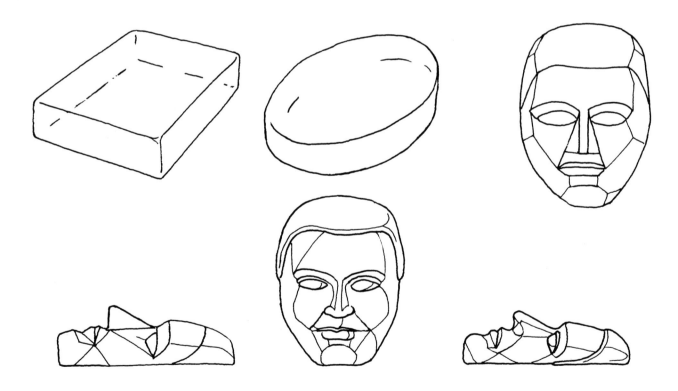

Project 16: Encaustic Panel Painting

It was a tradition in ancient Egypt to cover mummy cases with a portrait of the deceased. When Rome controlled Egypt, the tradition continued, but not the molded gold portraits of pharaohs. Instead, it was ordinary people who had their portraits painted with encaustic on wood panels, like that of a young woman shown here. Encaustic is a very permanent art technique, because the colors are melted wax painted on the panel. That is why these Egyptian portraits made during the Roman Empire 2,000 years ago survive today.

You can make an encaustic-type picture using wax crayons.

1. Select a piece of plywood or wood plank. Sand it smooth.

2. Create a design, similar to the portrait shown here. Draw your planned design onto the board with wax crayons.

3. As you work, blend the colors with the tip of a heated screwdriver. At the same time, smooth out the texture of the crayon drawing.

The wax-on-wood picture can be displayed by putting a screw eye in the upper middle of the back of the wood panel, and hanging it on the wall.

 Studio Projects in Art History

Project 17: Pompeii Wall Paintings

Homes with elaborately painted wall decorations have been found in the ancient Roman city of Pompeii, which was covered by an eruption of Mt. Vesuvius in A.D. 79. The decorations show scenes of mythology, daily life, landscapes, and cityscapes. Many look as if you are observing them through an opening between columns.

Below is a copy of some Pompeii wall paintings. The side panels illustrate two styles of imaginative city scenes. The buildings of one are piled together like toy blocks. The other is made up of temple columns. The framing columns and mask are also part of the decoration. In the empty space draw your own imaginative city scene, then color the complete wall design.

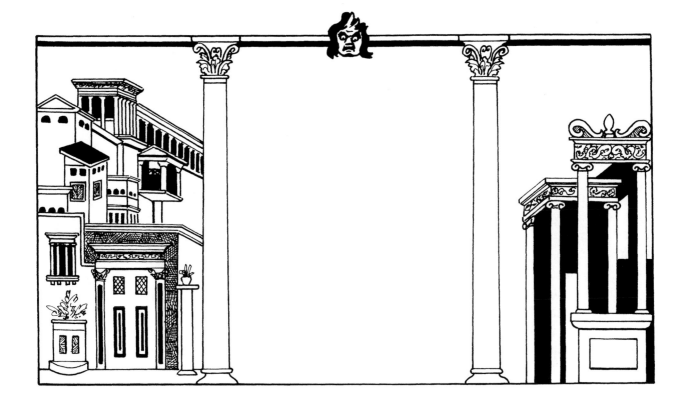

Project 18: Paper Roman Mosaic

The floors of Roman buildings were mosaic — small squares of tile (called *tesserae*) arranged into a picture. This street musician playing a tambourine copies a Roman mosaic. Use it to make a paper mosaic.

1. Select colored papers for your mosaic.

2. Cut the colored paper into ⅛″-wide strips.

3. Cut each strip into squares of about ⅛″.

4. Wipe stick paste on a small area of the picture.

5. Stick the proper color paper squares to the paste area with tweezers.

6. Roman artists made realistic mosaic pictures with shadows and high-lights. The thin lines of this copy mark shadow and highlight areas for your guidance.

7. The original colors were: hair and under-shirt yellowish with brown shadow; over-shirts green with yellow-green highlights; wrapped skirt red with pink highlights and brown shadow.

Project 19: Paper Roman Mosaic

Many Roman buildings had mosaic floors — small squares of tile (*tesserae*) arranged into a picture. This mosaic dog was a warning at the front door of an ancient Roman house. Use it to make a paper mosaic.

    1. Cut colored paper into ¼″ strips.

    2. Cut each strip into ¼″ squares.

    3. Wipe stick paste on a small area of the picture.

    4. Stick the paper tesserae to the paste area.

PART II:
MEDIEVAL ART

CHAPTER 7

Early Christian Art

Most students are familiar with two historical events which ushered in the era of Early Christian art: the fall of the Roman Empire and the beginnings of the Christian church. Like all significant changes in history, the change from one era to the other transpired over a period of time, long enough so anyone living during the period probably never noticed the change.

Christianity had been practiced in Rome and many of its provinces for decades before Emperor Constantine officially recognized it in A.D. 325. For political reasons he divided the Empire in two in 395, establishing his capital at Constantinople. Rome fell to the Visigoths in 410, and when Ravenna, Italy, fell in 476, the Western Roman Empire gasped its last breath.

Nevertheless, Constantinople survived as the greatest European capital for another 1,000 years, so for its people the Empire had never really fallen. The real transformation from one era to another, then, was not barbarians at the gates and degeneracy within. It was, instead, the gradual change of philosophical and cultural values, and the replacement of the worldly, humanistic culture of Classical Greece and Rome by the spiritual outlook of a new era which would become the Middle Ages.

The spiritual beginning of the Middle Ages expressed itself through art in two ways and in two places. The first was in the Early Christian art of the waning decades of the Empire, which adapted late Roman art to Christian themes. The second, not necessarily included with Early Christian art as a style, was the so-called "barbaric" style of northern Europeans — the Celts and Germanic tribes beyond the Empire's boundaries — and barbaric only in that its elaborate, abstract decoration was alien to Classical art. Three projects introduce these ideas to students. They can bring to them what they know of the early years of the Christian church, the catacombs, the fall of Rome, and the rise of Christianity as the dominating influence of the Western world.

Significant art dates:

Catacomb frescoes, third and fourth centuries
Old St. Peter's Cathedral, Rome, c. 333
Book of Lindisfarne, late seventh century
Book of Kells, eighth century

Early Christian Art
325–800

The earliest Christians practiced their religion in Rome and other cities of the Empire. Until Christianity was officially recognized, their art was small and private. They carried small devotional objects carved from wood or ivory. They painted pictures on the walls of their secret catacomb chapels. They used symbols in their art with religious meanings that authorities could not understand.

Centers of Early Christian art

Once Rome made the Christian church official, art served the new religion. The earliest styles were similar to the late Classical art of Rome. Christ appeared without a beard, for example, in Early Christian art. The illustration at right copies just such a carving representing Jesus. Classical symbols were used, such as the grapes of the Roman god of wine translated to the wine of the Last Supper and Holy Communion. Only gradually did styles change as artists began emphasizing the spiritual nature of Christianity while rejecting worldly Classical styles.

Christ Enthroned,
c. 359

Early Christian art from the northern British Isles

Roman occupation had never touched Ireland and Scotland in their remote corner of Europe. There, art consisted of intricate, abstract design. When the Christian religion reached them, the people of the northern British Isles adapted their decorative art to Christian themes, producing Early Christian sculpture, metal work, and manuscripts with no Classical Roman influence.

Student Name _____   Date _____

Project 20: Christian Symbolism

The earliest Christians in Rome had to worship in secret. In their art they used symbols which authorities could not understand but had meaning for church members. As centuries passed, many symbols were added to the early ones to identify saints and ideas for medieval persons who were unable to read. Here is a selection of Early Christian symbols. Search the decorations of local churches or examples of religious art to see which ones you can find, and identify their location.

Location:

 Red rose symbolizes *martyrdom*, white rose symbolizes *purity*.

 Vine symbolizes God's relation with His people, grapes the blood of Christ.

 Anchor is the symbol for *hope* and *steady faith*.

 Dove symbolizes *purity* and recalls the dove returning to Noah's ark.

(continued)

Project 20: Christian Symbolism *(continued)*

Location:

Whale with Jonah escaping from its belly symbolizes the *Resurrection.*

Lamb symbolizes *Jesus* (John 1:29) and Christ as the *Good Shepherd.*

Symbol for *Jesus* because letters of Greek word for *fish* stand for *Jesus Christ God's Son Savior.*

First two letters of *Christ* in Greek, *chi* (X) and *rho* (P), form this monogram cross.

First and last letters of Greek alphabet (*alpha* and *omega*) symbolize *Christ* as the beginning and the end (Rev. 1:8).

     Studio Projects in Art History

Project 21: Early Christian Diptych

Early Christian artists made diptychs — small, double-leafed hinged panels for private devotions. (Triptychs consisted of three leaves, the two wings folding over the center panel.) Many were carved in ivory, such as this sixth century diptych of St. Michael the Archangel. The other panel has been lost.

Make your diptych out of white plastic painted with black, gray, or dark brown acrylic paint.

1. Plan a design, copying this example or your original idea.

2. Cut two matching rectangles of white plastic. The original diptych is 5½″ by 17″, but you may cut pieces of a smaller, more convenient size.

3. Drill three holes along the edge of each plastic panel for the wire hinge.

4. Paint your design on the two plastic panels with acrylic paint, shading to give a three-dimensional effect.

5. Once the color has dried, hinge the two leaves together with small loops of wire.

(continued)

Project 21: Early Christian Diptych *(continued)*

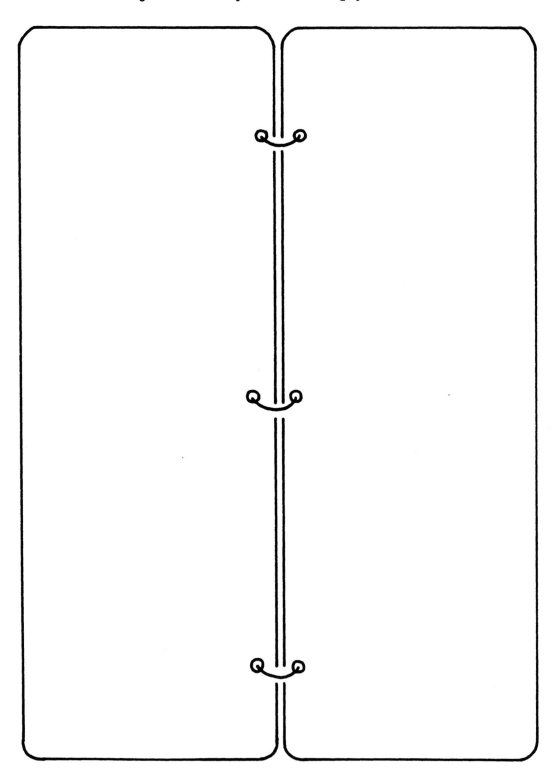

Project 22: Book of Kells

In the northern British Isles, monks in isolated monasteries created very intricate art in the sacred books they copied and decorated. This example is based on one richly colored, full-page-size initial letter from the *Book of Kells*, made in the eighth century. Make your own color selection as you enrich this letter design with color.

CHAPTER 8

Byzantine Art

Conventional Western history has focused on the medieval art of western Europe. Throughout that thousand-year period there was great art, literature, and philosophy being created in the Byzantine Empire of eastern Europe. Its importance in medieval Europe has made some historians speculate that Charlemagne thrived in the ninth century only because the Byzantine Empire was then internally weakened by the Iconoclastic Controversy. This political and theological debate was art-centered, since it involved the argument over the making of religious images.

Byzantine influence in western Europe later appeared as the model of much Romanesque art. In short, the thousand-year Byzantine Empire was of great historical importance and its art significant in its time and influential thereafter.

Of the great amount of Byzantine art, two kinds are most typical — icons and mosaics. Still painted today in Greece, Byzantine icons are the grandparents of the easel-painting tradition which has dominated art since the Italian Renaissance. Walls of Byzantine churches were completely covered with frescoes or mosaics. Never was the art of mosaic more gloriously practiced, the interior of St. Mark's in Venice being the most famous example.

Unfortunately, the great collections of Byzantine art are not in American museums (although it is fairly represented). However, Byzantine art remains alive in the Eastern Orthodox churches of our cities. If there are any local Greek, Russian, or Armenian churches, students can visit them to get a taste of Orthodox church art and see icons hanging on the iconostasis.

This chapter's three projects introduce icons and mosaics, the former in two projects. One explains the actual method of egg-tempera icon painting, which any interested student might try. The other, which describes a simpler method, may be more suitable to normal classroom situations.

Significant art dates:

Hagia Sophia, Constantinople, 532–537

San Vitale mosaics, Ravenna, c. 547

Daphne mosaics, Athens, eleventh century

St. Mark's, Venice, eleventh century

Andrei Rublev, Russian icon painter, c. 1370–1430

Byzantine Art
526-1453

When the Roman Emperor Constantine established a second capital which he named Constantinople (modern Istanbul), he laid the seed of the Byzantine Empire. For a thousand years after its founding, Constantinople flourished as one of the major cities of the Western world, the trading center between Europe and Asia, rich in buildings and art. With their themes almost exclusively religious, artists depicted their figures as tall and slim, staring as if looking at a spiritual vision rather than the mortal world. Such figures appeared in mosaics, wall frescoes, and icons.

Byzantine Empire

An icon, a painting on a wood panel, depicting Christ, Mary, or a saint, was hung in a church or home. Some church leaders argued that people might start worshipping icons instead of the holy persons they represented. Therefore, Emperor Leo III passed a law in 726 forbidding the making of icons. For over a century icons were forbidden in the Byzantine Empire. This was the Iconoclast period, a term meaning the "breaking of icons."

In the spring of 843 the Iconoclast Decree was lifted. Thereafter icons remained an important kind of Byzantine art, as were the frescoes and wall mosaics of churches. In 1453 Constantinople fell to the Ottoman Turks, bringing the Byzantine Empire to an end. Yet its religious spirit continues today in the Greek, Russian, and Armenian Orthodox churches, where icons still hang and fresco and mosaic decorations continue to brighten church interiors.

Project 23: Egg-Tempera Icon Painting

1. Sand the face of a sufficiently aged plank of wood about typewriter-page size. Apply gesso (available from art stores) to the sanded face in thin, diluted coats, up to ten. Stroke each coat of gesso in one direction only, alternating top-to-bottom and side-to-side, letting gesso dry between coats. (For example, brush the first coat from top to bottom, the second from side to side, then the third from top to bottom, and so on.) When the gesso has dried hard, draw the painting design on the panel with charcoal pencil.

2. Prepare the egg-tempera paint by diluting egg yolk with water so it flows with a brush but does not run freely. Add a couple of drops of vinegar. Only a bit of this solution is required for each color, so it is convenient to store in a small plastic container in the refrigerator.

3. Mix powdered tempera colors with the egg solution, adding enough water for a painting thickness. If you prefer tube tempera colors, add a few drops of the egg solution to the paint when working. With it the colors retain their brilliance.

4. First paint all flesh areas of the design with a pale yellowish-green color. When that has dried, paint highlighted flesh parts white. Paint all areas with their selected color. Paint over the greenish undertone with a thinned flesh tone, letting the greenish shading and the highlights show through to give dimension to the face and hands. Add details and shading as desired.

5. Purchase gold leaf from an art store. Apply as directed, using the adhesive recommended or sold with the gold leaf. Apply in one of two ways:

    1. Cut the design of the painting away from the gold sheet and apply as a single sheet to the background.

    2. Cut the gold leaf into small pieces and fix to the background around the design.

   The finished icon can be covered with artist's quality clear varnish.

Project 24: Modified Icon Painting

1. Select a plank of wood about typewriter-page size, aged enough so as not to warp or bleed resin. Sand the painting surface smooth. Brush diluted plaster onto the painting surface. This is similar to the gesso coating used in traditional icon painting. Once the plaster has dried, sand it smooth and apply a second coat, then sand smooth again.

2. Plan the design of the icon on a sheet of paper. Use carbon paper to transfer the design to the plaster-coated panel. Use tempera colors to paint the design, leaving the background empty.

3. When finished and dried, paint the background gold with hardware-store paint.

4. When the background has dried, cover the painted icon with clear varnish.

These copies of Byzantine icons can guide your design.

Project 25: Miniature Mosaic

The walls of many Byzantine churches were covered with brightly colored mosaics. Because of the church mosaics, there arose a popularity for miniature mosaics, pictures made of small colored cubes set in wax on a wooden panel.

1. To make yours, cut a piece of thin plywood 6″ by 8″.

2. Glue wood strips around the edges like a frame.

3. Varnish the frame strips a dark color.

4. Melt paraffin onto the plywood inside the frame.

5. Plan a mosaic design. The illustrated example copies a late twelfth-century Byzantine miniature.

6. Instead of the glass cubes of a Byzantine miniature mosaic, you can use the small beads used for bead craft. Using your plan as a guide, push the beads into the wax with the sides exposed, not the holes.

   Studio Projects in Art History

CHAPTER 9

Gothic Architecture

Perhaps there has never been a more successful religious architecture than the Gothic cathedral. It is difficult to demonstrate this success to students, for the Gothic cathedral's greatest glory is the soaring interior space duplicated in only a few nineteenth-century neo-Gothic cathedrals built in America. But the details of this expressive style can be delightful. The decorative stonework of pointed arch windows, the beauty of stained glass, and the whimsical monsters which perch as rainspouts along Gothic roof edges can be seen in many Gothic-revival buildings constructed in the mid-nineteenth century in the United States and Canada. Such Gothic details provide the subjects for this chapter's projects.

An architectural study sheet sends students looking for neo-Gothic details in older local buildings. They can make their own gargoyle rainspout—impractical on a modern building but fun as a study object. There are several ways to make a pseudo-stained-glass window. A project in the Walch book *100 Craft Projects from Around the World* uses cellophane to follow the traditional stained-glass-making procedure. This chapter's stained-glass window is simpler.

As a color guide, it can be noted that Chartres Cathedral glass is famous for blue backgrounds. Halos are of various colors besides yellow. The Virgin's robe is purple, symbolizing sorrow, and the hood blue, her traditional color. Or students can choose freely. The details of a Gothic cathedral are as subtle as the whole structure is inspiring; together they produce an aesthetic environment which expresses the beliefs (both superficial and profound), the dreams, and the realities of late medieval life.

Significant art dates:

Notre Dame Cathedral, Paris, 1163–1250   Cologne Cathedral, Germany, begun 1248
Chartres Cathedral, France, 1194–1220   Florence Cathedral, Italy, 1296–1436
Amiens Cathedral, France, 1220–1236   Milan Cathedral, Italy, begun 1386
Saint-Chapelle, Paris, 1243–1248   Burgos Cathedral, Spain, 1221–1568
Salisbury Cathedral, England, 1220–1270   Toledo Cathedral, Spain, begun 1227

**Regions of major
Gothic churches**

Gothic Architecture
1150–1500

The basic spirit of the one thousand years of the Middle Ages was religious. Therefore, the most important medieval art creation was the church building. All other arts were created to be part of it: sculpture and painting for its walls, music for its choirs, plays for performance in the square outside its doors. All medieval art served religion and its church building.

Byzantine domed churches were built in eastern Europe and the Middle East. As seen in the illustration here, in western Europe the first church style was Early Christian (1), a simple design developed from Roman architecture. By the year 1000 that style had developed into the Romanesque (2), a larger building with heavy stone walls, round arches and occasionally squat towers. By 1150 that style had changed into the Gothic (3) as builders discovered how to support high roofs atop a network of pointed arches, allowing the wall area between to be opened up for large windows. Colored glass in these window spaces let soft, tinted sunlight illuminate the Gothic interior.

Not only was the Gothic church richly decorated with art, but its decorative details, such as pointed arches and circular rose windows, became decorative motifs for other art objects. Gothic became the most spiritual of Christian art styles in the most religious period of Western culture.

Project 26: Gothic Architecture

With religion dominating life in medieval Europe, churches were the most important buildings in villages and cities. From 1150 to 1500 the expressive Gothic style was used for the design of these churches. It was again popular for nineteenth-century buildings, so you can find Gothic details in certain local churches. Here are some typical examples. Look for them in nineteenth-century buildings and note their location.

1. *arch:* Found as doors, windows, ceilings, and in decoration, the Gothic arch has a pointed top.

   Location: _____

2. *archivolt:* ornamentation around an arch

   Location: _____

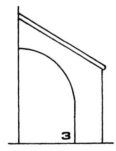

3. *flying buttress:* exterior wall support

   Location: _____

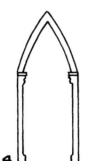

4. *lancet:* tall, narrow, pointed opening with no tracery

   Location: _____

(continued)

Project 26: Gothic Architecture *(continued)*

5. *quatrefoil:* decorative motif or frame with four equal petal shapes

   Location: _____

6. *rose window:* large, circular window of stained glass

   Location: _____

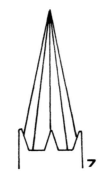

7. *spire* (or steeple): sharply angled pyramidal structure atop a tower

   Location: _____

8. *tracery:* interlaced branching decoration around a Gothic opening

   Location: _____

Project 27: Gothic Gargoyle

If you look at pictures of Gothic buildings, you may see stone monsters peering over the edges of the roofs. These creatures are actually the ends of rainspouts, carved so that during a rainstorm water streams out of their mouths. You can make a Gothic gargoyle, not for rain but for display.

1. Cut a section of plastic pipe 1″ to 2″ in diameter and 6″ to 8″ long.

2. Stick thumb tacks outward at one end of the pipe.

3. Build a ball about the size of a baseball of clay or Play-doh around that end of the tube.

4. Model and carve a monster's head into the clay ball so its mouth opens at the pipe end.

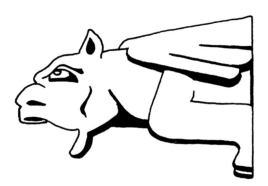

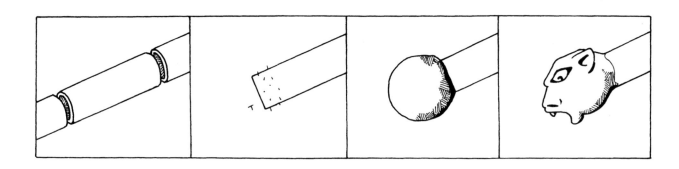

Project 28: Stained-Glass Window

This picture duplicates a thirteenth-century stained-glass window, *Death of the Virgin*, in the Cathedral of Chartres, France. Such windows were pieced together with colored glass held in place by strips of lead. Details were painted on the glass. Horizontal bars, two appearing here, gave added support.

1. Trace the picture on a sheet of tracing paper with a black felt pen.

2. Color your tracing with felt pens.

3. Cut a circular hole 5¼″ in diameter in a sheet of black construction paper.

4. Paste your colored tracing behind the hole and hang in a window.

CHAPTER 10

Medieval Decorative Art

The Middle Ages was an era when there was as yet no distinction between crafts and fine art. All objects, even such insignificant ones as door hardware, were created with a sense of art when made for medieval churches. Such are the study objects of this section.

Students cannot become medieval craftsmen. For them it is the aesthetic value of these objects which is important—the arrangement of jewels on a reliquary box, the composition of shapes and colors on a tapestry, and the shape of a metal fixture.

These objects were the creations of jewelers, weavers, and smiths. Projects can only simulate medieval decorative art. As students try these projects, they can discuss how the real object was made, what its original use was, and where it would have been used.

Significant art dates:

Bayeux Tapestry, c. 1073–1083
Nicholas of Verdun, enameled Klosterneuburg altarpiece, 1181
"Nine Heroes" Tapestry, c. 1380
"Hunt of the Unicorn" Tapestry, c. 1500

Medieval Decorative Art
800–1500

**Medieval
Europe**

Covered with sculpture and wall paintings, and graced with colorful stained-glass windows, medieval churches were great works of art in themselves. And they contained even more works of art, for they were treasuries of beautiful objects: jewel-encrusted gold and silver utensils and containers of sacred relics for altars; elaborate candlesticks for light; and decorative metal hardware for doors, windows, and furniture. The castles of royalty and nobility were just as richly furnished.

However, if medieval churches and castles were luxurious in their furnishings, they were not necessarily comfortable. The ceilings were high, the floors of cold stone or hard packed earth. Drafts blew through cracks in loosely fitted windows and doors. The central heating of castles was, at best, an open fireplace, and churches had no heat at all. To compensate, cold walls were hung with tapestries of heavy woven wool yarn depicting saints and legends. People wore thick clothing to keep warm in winter, royalty appearing splendid in richly embroidered and decorated fashions.

Many of these woven tapestries and jeweled gold and silver containers survive to delight us when visiting a museum of medieval art. They remind us of a time when craftsmen transformed useful objects into works of art.

Studio Projects in Art History

Project 29: Door Hardware

In the Middle Ages hardware was crafted by hand, often with as much a sense of art as utility. These examples are ornamental ironwork pieces. The strips, longer than illustrated, held together the heavy oak planks of church and castle doors. Use them as patterns and cut from the metal of large juice cans or other tin-can containers, preferably those with a gold-colored surface.

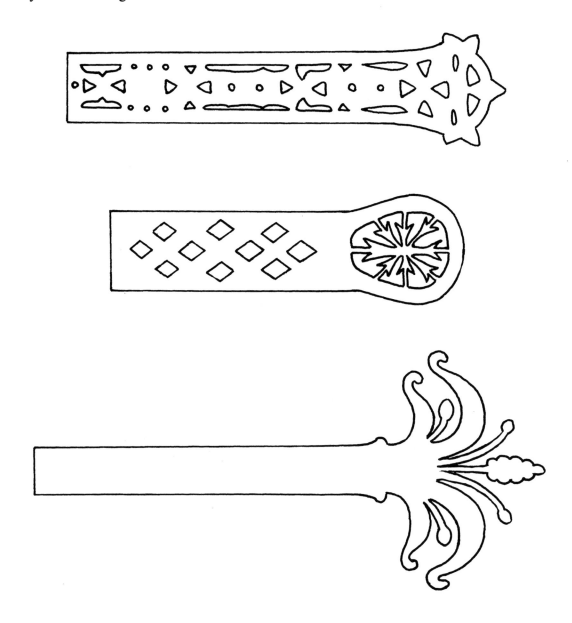

(continued)

Project 29: Door Hardware *(continued)*

You can also cut designs from metal foil and paste on notebook covers as decoration.

1. Cut away the lids and seam of the can with opener and shears, then flatten out.

2. Draw your design on the metal with a felt pen.

3. Cut out the design with tin snips or normal shears. Be careful of sharp can edges.

4. Tack the fixture to your bedroom door or mount it on a piece of dark varnished wood for display.

Project 30: Decorated Reliquary Box

The objects used in medieval church services — chalices (communion cups), patens (communion plates), aquamaniles (water containers) and reliquaries (boxes holding sacred relics) — were of gold or silver and decorated with jewels and enamel. Enamel is a brightly colored paste baked hard onto an object. The twelfth-century reliquary shown here is enameled with the symbols for the four Gospel writers (eagle: St. John; winged man: St. Matthew; lion: St. Mark; winged ox: St. Luke). Decorate a small box for holding coins or other objects.

(continued)

Project 30: Decorated Reliquary Box *(continued)*

1. Find a small plastic, wood, or metal box with lid.

2. Plan an appropriate design, using medieval motifs.

3. Paint the box with gold-colored paint.

4. Following your design, decorate with hobby enamel paint purchased from an art or hobby store.

5. If you wish, glue costume jewelry to the box.

Project 31: The Bayeux Tapestry

This very famous medieval tapestry is not a real tapestry; it is a 230-foot-long embroidery with pictures stitched in thread. After William the Conqueror invaded and occupied England in 1066 (one of the most important events in English history) the women of his court sewed the story of the conquest on this long, 20-inch-wide cloth with colored thread. Not only is it a unique piece of art, but it gives a wealth of visual information about military arms and armor, court fashions, construction methods, and habits of the eleventh century.

1. Cut a piece of cotton cloth to the proportions of this detail of the Bayeux Tapestry.

2. Thumbtack it to a drawing board or work table top.

3. Lightly copy the illustrated tapestry detail (or a design of your own) onto the cloth with a soft pencil.

4. Using different colors of thin felt-tipped pens, draw the Bayeux Tapestry detail on the cloth, using the pencil lines as a guide.

Student Name _____ Date _____

Project 32: Medieval Tapestry Collage

Cold medieval castle walls were hung with brightly colored tapestries illustrating religious themes and legends, such as this fourteenth-century tapestry of King Arthur. Rather than weaving a tapestry, make a cloth collage of a medieval subject, using this copy as a guide.

1. Collect pieces of scrap cloth.

2. Cut a piece of plywood or masonite to a convenient size (12″ x 15″, for example).

3. Plan a design which will utilize the cloth scraps.

4. Draw the design onto the plywood or masonite backing.

5. Cut the scraps to shape, then glue to the backing with white glue.

6. Draw details (faces, for example) on the cloth with felt-tipped pens.

7. Build up the design with cloth scraps, then display as a decorative hanging.

       Studio Projects in Art History

CHAPTER 11

Medieval Book Art

Only in rare cases is a book produced today as a work of art in itself. This was not the case in the Middle Ages, when a book was meant to be enjoyed by looking at it as much as by reading it. The reasons were twofold. One, virtually all books had a sacred purpose, for they were confined to religious subject matter for use in a church or for private devotions. Two, they were made by hand, carefully copied by monastery scribes from earlier copies. One can imagine medieval scribes, weary of copying every word by hand, turning with delight and sometimes with mischief to decorating margins and initial letters. In the finest examples, artists were employed to illustrate what scribes had copied. Throughout medieval Europe some of the most beautiful books ever made were produced.

These illuminated books were never larger than today's average book size and were frequently quite small, no more than three inches high. The illustrations were as a consequence tiny and precise, filled with detail for contemplation. This tradition led to the tiny background details such as rendering small objects from Late Gothic painting.

The three projects in this chapter represent medieval bookmaking. Students can design an initial letter for a text and make a Book of Hours, discovering how books were once fine art. A decorated cover suggests how sumptuous these books could be.

Significant art dates:

The Hours of Jeanne d'Evreux by Jean Pucelle, 1325–1328
Les Très Riches Heures du Duc de Berry, the Limbourg Brothers, 1413–1416

**Medieval
Europe**

Medieval Book Art
800–1500

uring the Middle Ages all books were written by hand, for printing was unknown in Europe. Most of them were copied by monks, though professional artists may have decorated them, for not only were texts written by hand, but pages were richly illustrated. Even pages devoted solely to written words had decorated initial letters beginning the page, frequently gilded. Such bright decoration reflected light as if it were illuminated, so medieval book decoration was called *illumination*. The decoration of this page is based on a thirteenth-century illumination.

Most of these illuminated books were made for churches or monasteries, but wealthy persons did own their own illuminated prayer books, small enough to carry in a pocket for travel. The pages of medieval books were made of parchment, which was sheep or goat skin. The covers were made of leather. Some books used in church services, especially those placed on altars, had covers of gold, silver, or ivory, enriched with jewels. Never have books been so beautiful as the hand-copied and hand-decorated books of the Middle Ages.

Student Name _____ Date _____

Project 33: Illuminated Manuscript Letter

edieval monks copied the pages of books by hand and richly decorated the more important pages of prayers, Biblical passages, or religious poems. The first letter of a page was enlarged and elaborated into a complex color design. Because gold was often used in the letter, it shone brightly, causing such text decoration to be called an *illumination*. Copies from two such letters in medieval manuscripts appear here.

esign and illuminate an initial letter from a religious selection of your choice in this empty square. Color it with felt-tipped pens or copy it on good drawing paper to paint, then hand-letter the text which follows it.

Project 34: Book of Hours

A Book of Hours was a hand-written and hand-decorated private prayer book, so named because it had special prayers for the hours of each church day. It also contained Biblical accounts, special devotions, and often a church calendar. This calendar noted the number of each of the days of the month, church festivals and holidays, and the divisions of the astrological year. The popularity of the Book of Hours began in the thirteenth century and continued into the fourteenth when some of the finest medieval artists created their small illustrations.

Make your own Book of Hours illustrations in a pocket notebook of unlined pages. The layout here, which you can use as a model, is based on the fourteenth-century *The Very Rich Hours of the Duke de Berry* by the Limbourg Brothers.

1. In the outer arc go the days of the month, 1 to 31.

2. In the next half-circle indicate holidays and festivals matched to the date.

3. The zodiac symbols for the month should appear on the starry sky, with their names on the inner half-circle. (For example: July's symbols would be a crab for Cancer and a lion for Leo.)

4. The framed space on the next page is for a drawing or photograph typical of the month's activities.

(continued)

Project 34: Book of Hours *(continued)*

Project 35: Decorated Book Cover

Books were so precious in the Middle Ages that some were given jeweled covers of gold or ivory. This was especially true of books used in churches, such as this illustrated example of the ninth century. Make your own cover, using the following instructions.

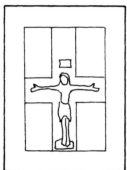

1. Cut a piece of heavy cardboard. The original cover of the illustration is 13¾″ by 10½″.

2. Create a design and draw it on the cardboard. Some of the design should be planned to stand in relief.

3. Tear newspaper into tiny bits and soak in water.

4. Take a small portion of the paper pulp, squeeze out excess water and mix with white (Elmer's) glue.

5. Shape and stick the pulp onto the design's relief parts.

6. When the pulp has dried, cut a sheet of thin gold foil or kitchen foil slightly larger than the cover.

7. Spread white glue over the cover. Lay the foil on the cover, pressing down to mold over the pulp relief.

8. When dry, decorate with costume jewelry or colored glass and paint details with acrylic paint.

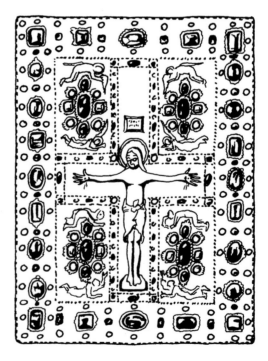

     Studio Projects in Art History

CHAPTER 12

Late Gothic Art

The fifteenth century was a watershed in art. Medieval in spirit, it was the starting place for most of the traditional methods of art practiced today. Painting on wood panels for display on church altars developed into modern easel painting. The oil-glaze technique introduced oil as a paint medium. Fifteenth-century woodcuts and engravings began the art of printmaking, which would eventually include lithography, etching, and other graphic techniques practiced today either as a fine art or commercial picture-reproducing methods. A transition period, Late Gothic art in northern Europe can be studied as the conclusion to medieval art or as a cultural partner with the fifteenth-century Italian Renaissance.

This chapter's projects are adapted to these fifteenth-century art methods. The oil-glaze project uses modern tube oil paint and a second modifies the oil-glaze technique even more for a still simpler experiment. Construction of altarpieces for student painting demonstrates panel painting, and woodcut printmaking is demonstrated in a simplified form. A final project introduces the special art of Hieronymus Bosch.

Significant artists:

Hubert and Jan van Eyck, c. 1390–1441
Rogier van der Weyden, c. 1400–1464
Hugo van der Goes, c. 1440–1482
Hans Memling, c. 1430–1495
Hieronymus Bosch, c. 1450–1516
Jean Fouquet, c. 1420–1481
Conrad Witz, c. 1400–1447
Martin Schongauer, c. 1445–1491

Late Gothic Art
1400–1500

**Flanders, France,
Germany, Switzerland**

In the late Middle Ages artists did not paint on stretched canvas as they do today. Instead, they painted on wood panels which were placed on church altars. However, in the early fifteenth century in Flanders, part of modern Belgium, artists began to take the steps leading to modern techniques by developing oil-glaze painting. By using slow-drying oil instead of quick-drying egg tempera, artists were able to blend colors, giving soft edges and rich shadows to a painting.

Among the first, if not the first, of Flemish artists to use oil paints were the Van Eyck brothers, Jan and Hubert. This illustration duplicates a painting by Jan van Eyck (c. 1390–1441), which some think may be his own self-portrait. Such worldly subjects as portraits were also a revolution, for medieval artists almost always had painted religious subjects. Not only were portraits now popular, but religious scenes were set in real landscapes, not unreal settings of gold. Artists were beginning to look at and record the world about them.

A Man in a Red Turban,
by Jan van Eyck

Fifteenth-century artists also made woodcut prints, pictures carved into wood blocks which were inked and then printed many times. Letter printing was also invented in this century. Ordinary people could now afford printed pictures for their walls and illustrated books for their homes. Oil-glaze painting, more worldly subjects, and woodcut prints helped usher in a new era as the Middle Ages were passing away.

Project 36: Oil-Glaze Technique

Until the early fifteenth century, artists painted with the egg-tempera technique. Then Late Gothic painters of Flanders began to use oil, rather than diluted egg yolk, to hold their pigments. Although modern oil painting developed from this beginning, the original oil-glaze technique differed considerably from modern practice. You can try this early method with these directions, modified to use modern tube oils.

1. Select a small board about typewriter-page size. Sand smooth.

2. Paint the sanded board with diluted gesso, available from art supply stores. Brush one coat with top-to-bottom strokes, the next coat with side-to-side strokes, and so on up to ten coats, letting dry between coats.

3. Plan a painting design, which in the Late Gothic era would have been a Madonna and Christ child, saint, or portrait.

4. Conceive the design in terms of light and shade.

5. Using oil paint from tubes, paint your design with shades of brown, tan, and white.

6. Allow the underpainting to dry, which can take several days. The structure of your composition is now in place. When dry, paint with oil paint *thinned* with linseed oil, glazing the surface of the painting with color. The underpainting shows through, giving shadow and dimension to the picture.

7. When dry, add any painted details you wish.

8. Cover the completed painting with clear varnish.

Project 37: Modified Glaze Technique

Use acrylic paints, which dry quickly, to create a Gothic-period glazed painting. In the late Middle Ages the subject would have been a portrait or a religious theme.

1. Paint on a small plank of wood, about typewriter-page size, aged enough not to warp or bleed resin. Sand it smooth.

2. If you do not use gesso, available from art supply stores, cover the painting surface with diluted plaster. Brush several coats onto the board, letting dry and sanding smooth between each. Alternate the application of plaster, one time vertically, one time horizontally.

3. Plan the design of your painting in terms of lights and darks on a sheet of paper. Copy the design on the gesso (plastered) panel.

4. Paint the design with acrylic paint, using shades of brown, tan, and white.

5. Once the brownish underpainting has dried, tint the surface with thinned acrylic colors. These colors can be brushed on the underpainting or applied with sponge, cloth, or the fingers. This glazing dyes the underpainting with color.

6. Details can be painted after the glazing has dried.

7. Cover the completed painting with clear varnish.

Project 38: Diptychs and Triptychs

Few medieval paintings were made to hang on walls. Instead, they usually stood on church altars. A double-winged altarpiece of two wood panels is called a *diptych*. With two paintings on equal-size wooden panels, you can make a diptych.

1. Buy two hardware-store hinges and attach the two panels.

2. Cut wood strips to size and frame each panel.

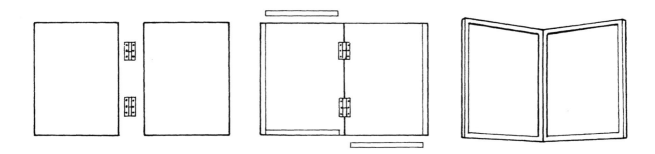

Triptychs were altarpieces of three sections, the two wings half the width of the center panel. The wings folded over the center panel, covering it during certain religious periods of the year. The backs of the wings had additional paintings exposed to view when they were closed. These back-of-wing pieces were often painted in grays to look like statues.

1. The panel paintings must be sized so the two wings are half the width of the center panel.

2. Hinge the three panels together.

3. Cut wood strips to size and frame the three panels.

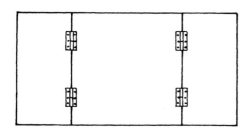  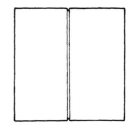

Project 39: Gothic Retable

Retables were elaborate constructions consisting of paintings or carvings placed on or behind church altars. The paintings or carvings were arranged in intricate gilded frames, such as this example. Color this frame gold or yellow. Collect greeting cards with religious themes, cut to shape, and paste in the empty spaces.

Project 40: Simple Woodcut Print

In the Late Gothic fifteenth century, European artists began making woodcut prints. The illustration copies an early example. You make a woodcut by printing from a block of wood (or linoleum block) into which you have cut a picture design.

1. Sand the surface smooth if using a wood block.

2. Cut a V-shaped groove around the design with a hobby knife as in Figure 2.

3. Cut away any areas between the grooves which are to be white in the print. Leave uncut the raised areas which will be printed black.

4. If woodcut printing is available, ink the raised portion of the block with an inking roller. If not available, brush acrylic paint directly from the tube over the raised portions of the block.

5. Lay a sheet of paper over the inked block. Holding it in place, rub the back of the paper in a circular motion with the bottom of a tablespoon.

6. Once inked, lift the paper from the block to dry.

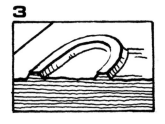

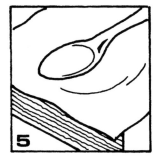

Project 41: The Art of Bosch

Hieronymus Bosch (c. 1450–1516) was a special sort of Gothic artist, filling his religious paintings with imaginative creatures, winged fish, people with heads of fruit, animals with musical-instrument noses, and many more. Some of his weird beings perch atop this frame. Using your imagination, invent similar creatures and objects within the empty frame. You can also cut portions of magazine pictures and paste them here in odd combinations to create an imaginative vision of paradise or the underworld, two subjects Bosch often painted.

 Studio Projects in Art History

PART III:

RENAISSANCE AND BAROQUE ART

CHAPTER 13

Italian Renaissance

The outlook of Renaissance art remained basic to Western art until the twentieth century. The humanistic philosophy of Renaissance art contrasted sharply with the medieval emphasis on religion in all aspects of life. Only with such a humanistic attitude could the philosophical and scientific progress of the Renaissance and subsequent centuries take place.

In art, the Renaissance rediscovery of the Classical past is most clearly seen in the adoption of ancient themes and styles—the use of Classical architectural devices in Renaissance building design, the application of Greek proportions and postures to the figures of paintings and statues, and the new fashion for mythological subjects in paintings. (Students can review Greek figure proportions and contrapposto posture in Project 13 of Chapter 5.)

The first project of this chapter shows how Renaissance painters, influenced by Classical statues, gave their figures a solid, sculpturesque appearance. The idealism, serenity, and stability of Classical art were characteristic of Italian Renaissance art, seen in the formal arrangements preferred by painters of the period. The Renaissance triangle, for example, is a very stable form, with a broad base and central emphasis. It is the composition of countless Renaissance paintings of the Madonna and Holy Family. It also demonstrates to students that composition (the arrangements of the parts in a picture) is not haphazard, but planned for a purpose — in the case of the Renaissance, for formality and stability.

Linear perspective — invented and sometimes excessively exploited in the Renaissance — also contributes to this formal arrangement by placing objects on a very strict grid. The Early Renaissance preference for one-point rather than two-point perspective accentuated this formality even more. For students, perspective projects are most interesting for their means of visualizing three dimensions on a two-dimensional surface. Renaissance painters were similarly intrigued.

Significant artists:

Early Renaissance	High Renaissance	Venetian Renaissance
Tommaso Masaccio, 1401–1428	Leonardo da Vinci, 1452–1519	Gentile Bellini, 1429–1507
Paolo Uccello, 1397–1475	Raphael Sanzio, 1483–1520	Giovanni Bellini, c. 1430–1516
Fra Angelico, 1387–1455	Michelangelo (Buonarrotti),	Giorgione, c. 1478–1511
Andrea Mantegna, 1431–1506	1475–1564	Titian, 1477–1576
Sandro Botticelli, 1444/5–1510		Tintoretto, 1518–1594

Italy in Europe

Italian Renaissance
1400–1600

For one thousand years the art of ancient Greece and Rome had lain in neglect, most of it destroyed. Then fifteenth-century Italian artists began to look at the Classical art still surviving in their country, giving a rebirth to those ancient ideas and styles. *Renaissance* means rebirth, and the fifteenth century was indeed born again to the more worldly, humanistic cultures of ancient Greece and Rome. The period did not reject Christianity, but it gave human beings more control over their own destiny.

Renaissance artists adopted Classical subjects and styles in their work, as in Sandro Botticelli's (1444/5–1510) *Birth of Venus*, its main figure shown here. They even made Christian saints look like Classical statues, using ancient posture and proportions to depict human figures. Classical ideas merged with Christian philosophy.

Because they wanted the figures and objects of their paintings to appear as if they existed in a real world, Renaissance artists eagerly took up the linear-perspective system invented by the architect Filippo Brunelleschi (1377–1446). This meant arranging the objects of a picture on imaginary lines which converged on a point on the horizon line. Linear perspective leads to a stable, formal kind of picture. Of course, Classical art had been formal and stable, favoring a strong central emphasis in a composition. Renaissance artists arranged their paintings in the same way, adopting triangular compositions and other devices to create noble art for serious contemplation.

Studio Projects in Art History

Project 42: Shading for Solidity

With their wish to make subjects appear more natural, Early Renaissance artists wanted to paint figures which appeared solid — three-dimensional rather than flat. Taking Greek and Roman sculpture as their model, they used ancient figure proportions and made them appear statuesque with the technique of shading. By imagining a light source from one side and casting the other side in shadow, Early Renaissance painters made their subjects appear to have the solidity of statues.

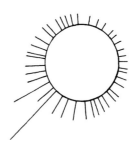

This figure duplicates a detail in a fresco by Tommaso Masaccio (1401-1428), the earliest artist to paint in a Renaissance style. Imagine a light source from the right and shade this figure to give it a solid, statuesque appearance.

Project 43: Linear Perspective

Using one-point perspective to create an illusion of three-dimensional space, an artist places objects on lines which meet at a central point on the picture's horizon line. This system was invented and used extensively in the Italian Renaissance. Perugino (1450–1523) even painted perspective lines in the pavement of his *Christ Delivering the Keys of the Kingdom,* diagrammed here. Design an appropriate subject in the frame below, using the perspective lines to arrange your composition.

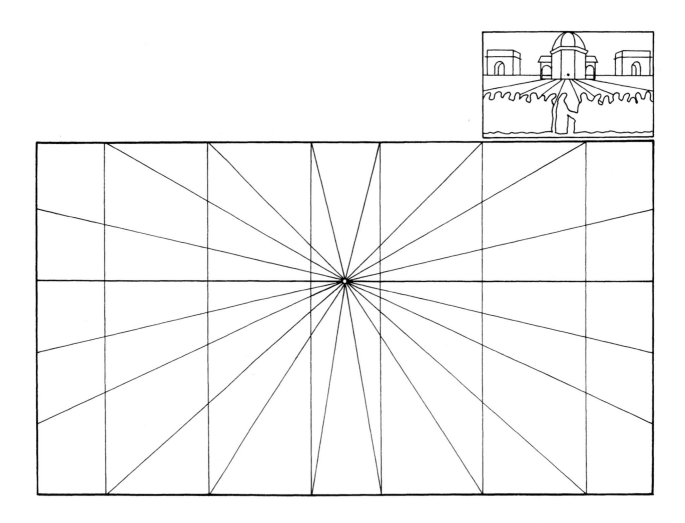

Project 44: Foreshortened Figures

Many Renaissance artists delighted in testing their ability with perspective by arranging figures in odd positions seen from awkward viewing angles. These two foreshortened figures are copied from Luca Signorelli's (1445–1523) *The End of the World*. Using them and perhaps class members as models, draw a foreshortened figure in the frame below.

Project 45: Renaissance Triangle

Italian Renaissance artists arranged their paintings in a triangular composition so often that it has become known as the *Renaissance triangle*. You see it in paintings of the Madonna and Christ Child, such as the one by Giovanni Bellini (c. 1430–1516) illustrated here. Any subject with a taller central figure above one or between two lower figures produces a stable, formal, broad-based composition. Conceive a picture idea which fits figures onto this triangle.

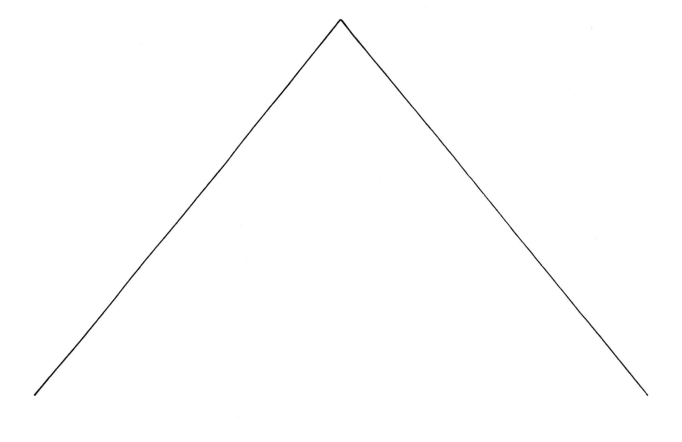

Studio Projects in Art History

Student Name _____   Date _____

Project 46: Renaissance Tondo

The Renaissance was one of the rare times when a circular picture, called a *tondo,* was popular. With all edges equidistant from its center, a tondo arrangement is very formal. It is also a difficult composition because there is no particular base, top, or sides to fit into. Renaissance artists painting a tondo usually imagined a tipped rectangle composition superimposed on the circle, such as Raphael's (1483–1520) *Madonna of the Chair.*

Arrange a picture in the tondo frame below.

Project 47: Fresco Cartoon

This picture has been copied from Michelangelo's (1475–1564) Sistine Chapel frescoes in the Vatican. Many familiar Italian Renaissance pictures are frescoes, which are large paintings on church or palace walls. Artists paint frescoes on wet, fresh plaster, which absorbs the colors, making the picture as permanent as the wall. The artist must work rapidly before the plaster dries, and he cannot make changes. Therefore, the artist first makes a full-size drawing of the design, called a *cartoon,* which is then transferred to the wet plaster. Most Renaissance artists transferred cartoon designs with pin holes, a method you can practice with this drawing.

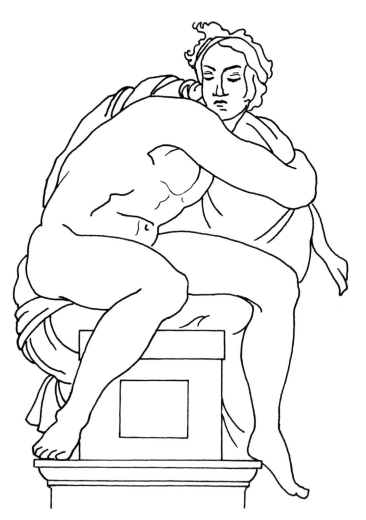

1. Trace the drawing on a sheet of tracing paper.

2. Prick holes with a pin around the traced drawing and along the lines of details.

3. Tape the pin-pricked tracing over a sheet of paper, painting canvas, or wall.

4. Use cotton to powder charcoal, powdered paint, or soot over the pinholes.

5. Remove the tracing paper. Connect the powdered dots on the paper, canvas, or wall with a pencil.

6. Complete the picture, following the penciled plan.

         Studio Projects in Art History

CHAPTER 14

Leonardo da Vinci

The High Renaissance in Italy, in the half century after 1480, produced three rare geniuses: Raphael, Michelangelo, and Leonardo da Vinci. In our century Raphael's art has lost some of its glitter, but the work of the other two is as greatly admired as ever.

This chapter takes Leonardo as the culmination of the Renaissance artist and personality. The variety of Leonardo's accomplishments is not only impressive, it inspires projects which can serve as examples of the multi-talented individual of the Renaissance.

Each project differs significantly from the others, in the same way that Leonardo's many projects seemed at times to have little relation to each other. His famous notes contribute to all but one of the projects. His visual observations are valid art lessons, and his inventions show that creativity is not confined to art alone. Leonardo's painting is represented by one of his unfinished works, demonstrating that in the High Renaissance color was of less importance than structure and shape. Let Leonardo da Vinci represent the Renaissance spirit at its most sublime.

Significant dates:

St. Jerome, c. 1481
The Last Supper, 1497
Virgin and Child with St. Anne, c. 1506–1510
Mona Lisa, 1513–1515

Leonardo da Vinci
1452–1519

**Leonardo in
Italy and France**

The Renaissance had many fine artists, but, along with Michelangelo, the greatest was Leonardo da Vinci. Only fourteen paintings by this Renaissance genius survive: most are unfinished and it is not certain that he painted all of them. Among them are his *Mona Lisa* and *The Last Supper*, two of the world's most famous paintings.

Leonardo da Vinci

The reason Leonardo never did many paintings, and few statues (none of which survive) is that his restless energy led him from one project to another. Painter, sculptor, and architect, he was also an inventor, engineer, scenic designer, botanist, and art theorist, and was hired at one court as a singer. Many persons of the Renaissance displayed talent and knowledge in several areas, but none could compete with Leonardo da Vinci in such a diversity of interests. He was the supreme example of the Renaissance person.

Leonardo's life was as restless as his projects. Born in the small Tuscan village of Vinci, he lived and worked in Florence, Milan, and Rome. Recognizing his genius, Francis I of France invited him to his court, where Leonardo da Vinci died away from his native Italy. He had observed the world with the mind of a scientist and the eye of an artist, demonstrating that the two can work together to create lovely art.

Project 48: The Unfinished *St. Jerome*

Influenced by sculpture, Renaissance artists thought more in terms of solid shapes: therefore they composed with light and shade rather than color. Leonardo da Vinci left two paintings unfinished in the first-stage monochrome, brownish color. Many experts feel he went no further for fear that color would detract from the basic solidity of his composition.

Now you finish this 500-year-old composition of *St. Jerome in the Wilderness.* First shade, then color. In the original *St. Jerome,* the lion and two background spaces beyond the rocks are light in tone, the rest dark.

Project 49: From Leonardo's Notes

Leonardo da Vinci filled many notebooks with his observations and ideas. Here are some of his notes which apply to art. Select one and create a picture on the back of this sheet which uses his suggestion.

1. Shadow is the means by which bodies display their form.

2. The conditions of shadow and light seen by the eye are three. The first is when the eye and the light are on the same side of the object seen. The second is when the eye is in front of the object and the light is behind it. The third is when the eye is in front of the object and the light is on one side.

3. When walking, a man has his head in advance of his feet.

4. The colors of the shadows in mountains seen at a great distance take on a beautiful blue. Considering this, it follows that when distant mountain rock is reddish, the illuminated parts appear violet.

5. A dark object seen against a bright background appears smaller than it is. A light object looks larger when seen against a background darker than it is.

6. If you wish to make an imaginary animal appear natural, for example a dragon, take for its head that of a hound with the eyes of a cat, a porcupine's ears, a greyhound's nose, the brow of a lion, the temples of an old rooster, and the neck of a turtle.

7. Old men should be shown with slow and heavy movements, and, when they stand still, their legs bend at the knees with feet placed apart, the head leaning forward and their arms extended very little.

Project 50: Leonardo's Wing Machine

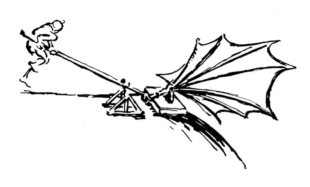

Among the ideas Leonardo da Vinci included in his many pages of notes was a machine for testing the lifting power of a wing. Make a model of this device by cutting out the 5 pieces, folding and gluing with stick glue as shown in Figure 1. Cut 3 match sticks ¾″ long to project through the rings and holes as hinges, assembling the wing machine as in Figure 2. The uprights of the two bases can be held by a strip of scotch tape.

(continued)

Project 50: Leonardo's Wing Machine *(continued)*

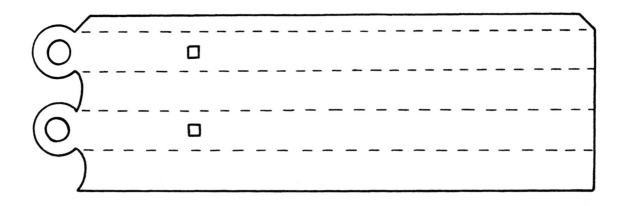

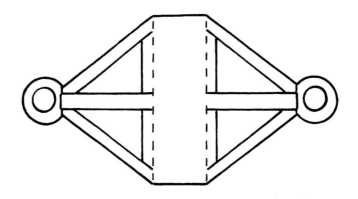

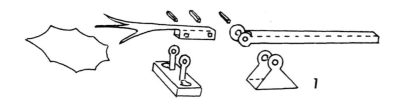

1

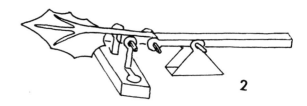

2

Project 51: Leonardo's Inventions

Throughout his life, Leonardo da Vinci kept journals in which he kept his ideas and observations about art and other pursuits. These notebooks included ideas for machinery which his active mind invented. Many of these ideas became actual machines 500 years later, in the twentieth century.

Here are copies of some of Leonardo's invention ideas. Select one and use cardboard, paper, string, glue — whatever you need — to make a model of a Leonardo invention.

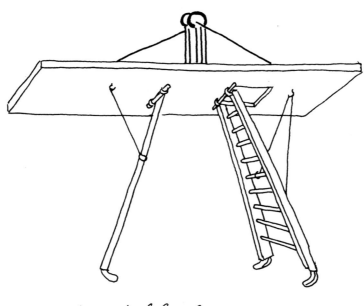

retractable ladder for an aircraft

(continued)

Project 51: Leonardo's Inventions *(continued)*

armored tank

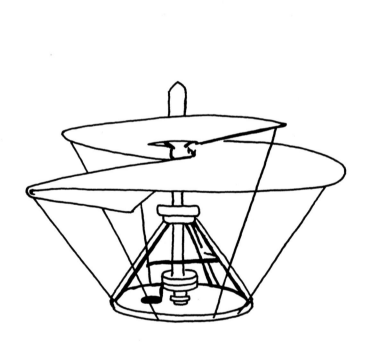

helicopter

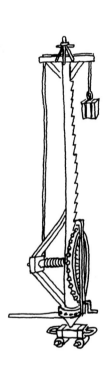

construction crane

CHAPTER 15

Northern Renaissance Art

The definition of Northern Renaissance art, that which was produced north of the Alps in the sixteenth century, is Italian Renaissance ideas overlaying Late Gothic themes and styles. The art of Dürer demonstrates this mix, as he portrays religious figures posturing in Renaissance contrapposto but with an angular, linear quality that recalls Gothic art.

The themes of Northern Renaissance art are similar to those of Italy, but the religious subjects have a more passionate tone, and mythological scenes are set in a Black Forest environment rather than on sunny Mediterranean slopes. It is wise to remind students that this is the time of the Protestant Reformation in central Europe. Dürer was a contemporary of Luther, his native Nuremberg the first city to become Protestant, and Luther noted the passing of the artist upon Dürer's death. Holbein painted portraits of Erasmus, Sir Thomas More, and King Henry VIII, all leading figures of the era's religious debates.

Northern Renaissance art looked ahead as much as it recalled the past. Pieter Bruegel was among the first to paint landscapes. His paintings of peasants enjoying everyday life led to the genre art of the following century. His down-to-earth realism, counter to the idealism of the Italian Renaissance, would influence the cult of naturalism in subsequent northern European art. All three of these artists are represented in the projects of this chapter, as the Renaissance in the north was a mingling of past, present, and future in art. And the future would belong to northern Europe, as in the coming centuries the centers of art would be found north of the Alps.

Significant artists:

Albrecht Dürer, 1471–1528
Lucas Cranach the Elder, 1472–1553
Matthias Grünewald, c. 1475–1528
Hans Holbein the Younger, 1497/98–1543
Jean Clouet, c. 1485–1540
Pieter Bruegel the Elder, c. 1520?–1569

Northern Renaissance Art
1500–1600

Major Northern Renaissance countries

By 1500 the ideas of the Italian Renaissance had begun spreading beyond the Alps into northern Europe, especially Germany, France, and the Lowlands. The German Albrecht Dürer (1471–1528), one of the first to adopt the new ideas, began as a Gothic-style artist. After a stay in Venice where he saw the Italian Renaissance in full flower, he developed his own Renaissance style in woodcuts, engravings, and paintings. His work ranks him as a Renaissance master.

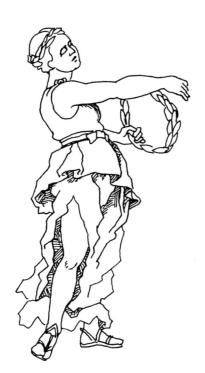

Northern Renaissance art combines Italian Renaissance theories with a lingering medieval Gothic spirit. The figure on this page, copied from a detail of a Dürer woodcut, shows this combination at work. Its dress and contrapposto stance is typical of the Italian Renaissance. However, the heavy peasant appearance of the model is more like the naturalism of the Late Gothic style.

Another German, Hans Holbein the Younger (1497/98–1543), used Renaissance realism in the many portraits he painted, but used a medieval theme, "The Dance of Death," for his important series of woodcuts. Pieter Bruegel the Elder (1520–1569) used Renaissance naturalism, but gave his figures a very northern appearance.

This was the period of the Protestant Reformation in Germany. Dürer followed the Reformation ideas of his countryman Martin Luther. Once he left Germany, Holbein's chief patron was Henry VIII, who introduced the Reformation to England. It was a period of great change, in philosophy as well as art.

     Studio Projects in Art History

Project 52: Dürer's Religious Prints

The greatest artist of the Renaissance in northern Europe was the German Albrecht Dürer (1471–1528). Besides his excellent paintings, he designed woodcuts and engraved prints, several as a series of pictures illustrating a particular Biblical story. For example, Dürer's *Great Passion* depicted events in the Crucifixion and Resurrection of Christ. The woodcuts of that series are: *The Last Supper, Christ on the Mount of Olives, Christ Taken Captive, Whipping of Christ, Christ Before the People, Christ Bearing the Cross, The Crucifixion, Mourning for Christ, Entombment, Christ in Limbo, The Resurrection.*

Dürer made four other series illustrating the Passion of Christ, plus a series of the life of the Virgin Mary and another illustrating the Revelations of St. John.

Select some Biblical or other religious narrative with which you are familiar. Write the title on the line, and in the boxes sketch or name the events you would choose to illustrate the series.

Project 53: Holbein's *Dance of Death*

Because of wars, famine, and epidemics, death was a frequent visitor in the Middle Ages and Renaissance. One popular theme of the era was the "Dance of Death" in literature and art. In art it showed death, represented by a skeleton, appearing to people. The theme reached a climax during the Northern Renaissance when Hans Holbein (1497/98–1543) designed a series of woodcut prints depicting the Dance of Death. The copy, drawn here in the size of the original, depicts death appearing to a doctor who expects to see a patient.

In each print the person is engaged in a typical activity when death appears. Besides the doctor, other woodcuts feature an emperor, king, cardinal, empress, queen, bishop, duke, nobleman, judge, advisor, preacher, priest, old wife, astronomer, rich man, businessman, sailor, soldier, count, duchess, merchant, plowman, and young child.

Not all these subjects would fit today's world, and there are modern professions not found in Holbein's series. On the lines below list persons whom you think would appear in a modern "Dance of Death" picture. Select one and make a drawing in the empty frame, using the copy of *The Doctor* as a guide.

The Doctor

Project 54: Bruegel's *Land of Plenty*

Three men lie beneath a tree, weary from work and dreaming of an effortless land where eggs present themselves ready-cooked, chickens willingly lay their heads on plates, pigs run about sliced for eating, pies lie on a shed roof, and a fence is made of linked sausages. This is what Pieter Bruegel (c. 1520?–1569) imagined in his painting *Land of Plenty.*

Add more to this dreamland picture, making life even easier for these three idlers.

CHAPTER 16

Baroque Art

The noble conceptions of the Renaissance made follow-up difficult; Renaissance art could be used as a model, but never equaled. It was necessary to depart from what the Renaissance had achieved without rejecting its basic principles. This is what the seventeenth-century artists of the Baroque set out to do. Where there had been stability and formality, they introduced movement and action. Where there had been sophisticated idealism, they introduced dramatic emotion. They replaced interest in structure with interest in color and light. While they continued in the tradition of painting religious subjects, mythological events, and portraits, they added landscapes, still lifes, and genre subjects to the painter's repertoire.

Baroque art can be divided roughly into two manners. The first was most frequently found in Catholic Europe, with the exception of Spain. Its precursor was Rubens with his large, action-filled canvases. Classical reserve modifies French Baroque, but its extravagant spirit is the essence of the reign of Louis XIV. The second Baroque manner was found in The Netherlands and will be dealt with in the next chapter.

The first project in this chapter is inspired by a painting by Rubens. Students are asked to complete a Rubens composition by drawing one part and then passing it on. Let students add to the story of the falling Arab (falling off a horse while being mauled by a lion in the original) without any guidance. Or, tell them that the Arab is the central figure in Rubens' *The Lion Hunt*. Emotions, light, and more drama complete the projects.

If not always attuned to modern tastes, the Baroque art of Rubens and his many followers speaks of the seventeenth century when Versailles and palaces patterned after it were built throughout Europe, with elaborate statues, and hung with large, dramatic compositions. The enthusiasm for such extravagant art can be compared to our modern taste for the exciting visual effects of movie spectaculars.

Significant artists:

Peter Paul Rubens, 1577–1640
Frans Snyders, 1579–1657
Jacob Jordaens, 1593–1678
Anthony van Dyck, 1599–1641

Georges de La Tour, 1593–1652
Nicolas Poussin, 1594–1665
Claude Lorrain, 1600–1682
Charles Lebrun, 1619–1690

Baroque Art
1600–1750

Baroque Europe

Baroque artists filled their paintings with action, drama, and emotion. Even Baroque skies are tossed with thunder clouds and light. Flowers and foliage ripen as decoration. Figures — seldom still — stretch, move, and gesture. Whether it is a religious subject, a mythological theme, a battle, a lion-hunting scene in North Africa, or a portrait, this art is dramatic and exciting.

This is the typical Baroque style, first fully rendered in the paintings of Peter Paul Rubens (1577–1640). Although it was not the only Baroque style,  in the seventeenth century Rubens' Baroque manner was seen in the art of most Catholic countries: Flanders, France, Italy, Austria, and southern Germany.

For added drama, Baroque artists painted light into their compositions. Light made a stormy sky stormier, a twilight landscape more dramatic. The light of some Baroque paintings acts like a spotlight, picking out carefully painted, realistic details, giving the appearance of three dimensions while casting parts of a picture into mysterious shadow. Baroque paintings, statues, and buildings come to you with all of the drama of an elaborate theatrical production.

Project 55: Rubens' Workshop

Peter Paul Rubens (1577–1640) painted large Baroque canvases filled with action and emotion. They were as visually exciting as a modern movie spectacular. He painted so many that others collaborated with him, completing paintings executed to Rubens' designs. Frans Snyders (1579–1657) specialized in animals, Anthony van Dyck (1599–1641) in portraits, and Jacob Jordaens (1593–1678) in robust figures. Each of them went on to become established Baroque painters in their own right.

In the frame below you will work as one of Rubens' assistants. The figure in the center is taken from a Rubens painting. In one of the dotted areas draw in more of the picture as you imagine it. Then pass it on to a classmate to develop another section, continuing until the frame contains a complete picture.

Project 56: Facial Expressions

Charles Lebrun (1619–1690), a court painter for France's King Louis XIV, designed all the decoration in the Palace of Versailles — everything from the paintings on the walls to the locks on the doors. He was also Director of the French Academy of Art, where he laid down principles which lasted for generations.

These six heads copy examples of facial expressions which Lebrun drew for students. Depicting emotions was important in the drama of Baroque art. Use these seventeenth-century examples as models when drawing faces of two different expressions in the frames below. The emotions depicted here are (from left to right, top to bottom) sadness, laughter, fear, anger, uneasiness, depression. Label your two expressions.

_____   _____

Project 57: Baroque Ceiling Fresco

Baroque artists delighted in creating theatrical effects. Most dramatic are the ceilings of Baroque churches in which perspective and light and shadow make the painting of a flat ceiling appear as if the roof has opened and you are looking up at some dramatic event in the sky.

These two people are painted in the corner of a ceiling in a German church. In the original they are looking in wonder at the Madonna enthroned. You can supply a different subject, if you wish, in the empty work space. Your drawing should relate to the two figures already in place, and your subject should appear as if it is floating above you.

Studio Projects in Art History

Project 58: La Tour's Light

Baroque artists used light in various ways for visual effects in their paintings. Georges de La Tour's (1593–1652) approach was to illuminate a scene with a concentrated, single light source, such as a torch or candle. This threw some areas into deep shadow and brightly illuminated others, as in the smaller drawing of his painting *The Magdalene* to the left. Such lighting is very dramatic, while giving a strong sense of clean form and emphasizing details such as wrinkles and folds of cloth standing out against the dark shadows.

The drawing on the right duplicates La Tour's painting of *St. Joseph, the Carpenter:* Jesus as a young boy holds a candle for his working father. The original painting is very dark, with the boy's face the most brightly lit by candlelight. Shade this drawing, thinking carefully about which areas must be left unshadowed because of the candle illumination.

     Studio Projects in Art History

CHAPTER 17

Dutch Baroque Art

The seventeenth century was the golden age of Dutch painting, with Frans Hals, Rembrandt, and Jan Vermeer the brightest gilt. Dutch Baroque art differs from the "typical" Baroque of Rubens. It is calmer, less colorful, and less subject to fantasy. Instead, it stresses realism in subject and style. However, like the Rubens Baroque, it is an outgrowth of Renaissance ideas, rendering natural appearances in as realistic a manner as possible.

Devoting a special chapter to the Dutch makes it seem that realistically styled genre, portrait, and landscape art was confined to Holland. Actually, the Dutch Baroque manner also appeared in Catholic and royalist France and Spain, but the Dutch masters best define this sort of art in the seventeenth century.

Freed from the traditional patronage of church and court due to the political and religious nature of Protestant Holland, Dutch artists had to find other support. It came in private sales and commissions to merchant families initiating the modern methods of art economics. Working alone, and not for the satisfaction of insistent patronage, Dutch artists became individuals in styles and manners of living. They also suffered the whims of the marketplace: Rembrandt was forced into bankruptcy, Hals ended life in a poorhouse, and Vermeer was forgotten soon after his death, all fates which would from now on befall many artists.

The projects in this chapter address the subjects which Dutch artists painted — landscapes, genre, still lifes, and portraits. They are adapted to give students some insight into how the Dutch Baroque artists handled these subjects.

Significant artists:

Frans Hals, c. 1580–1666
Rembrandt van Rijn, 1606–1669
Pieter Claesz, c. 1597–1661
Jan Vermeer, 1632–1675
Gerard Ter Borch, 1617–1681
Jacob van Ruisdael, 1628/29–1682

Student Name _____   Date _____

**Holland
in Europe**

Dutch Baroque Art
1600–1700

Dutch art of the seventeenth century was not the elaborate Baroque of Rubens in Flanders. Instead, it was a relatively calm, realistic view of the world Dutch artists knew. Holland was the first democracy of modern Europe, and its Protestant beliefs discouraged religious art. As a result, the Catholic Church and a royal court, the traditional patrons of art, were not available to Dutch painters. Their support came instead from the merchant middle class which came to prosperity in seventeenth-century Holland.

The art subjects which these middle-class Protestants preferred were things they saw around them. They wanted portraits of themselves. They also liked genre paintings — pictures of ordinary people in everyday life situations, as shown in this copy of Jan Vermeer's (1632–1675) *Woman Weighing Gold.* Dutch artists also painted landscapes — the flat countryside around their towns and the sea which slapped at their dikes. And they painted still lifes — arrangements of fruit, flowers, glassware, bottles, and silver which decorated the homes of the middle class.

These proud merchants, controlling their own destinies, free of the dogma of court and church, disliked the Baroque excesses of their neighbors. They preferred paintings which appeared as realistic as possible. Such a conservative outlook did not hurt the progress of art, for among Dutch Baroque painters were Jan Vermeer and Rembrandt, two of the greatest artists who ever lived.

Project 59: Genre Art

Art lovers in the seventeenth century enjoyed the *genre painting*, a picture in a realistic style which showed ordinary people in everyday activities: sitting in a tavern, having a tooth pulled, playing cards, sewing, taking a music lesson, and so on. Lightly outlined in this frame is *The Suitor's Visit* by Gerard Ter Borch (1617–1681) in which a young man comes courting to a Dutch home and is greeted by his girlfriend while another couple enjoys music by a fireplace. Using a felt-tip pen, bring the scene up to date, giving it a twentieth-century atmosphere and dress.

Project 60: Self-Portrait

During his lifetime Rembrandt (1606–1669) painted many self-portraits, showing himself in different stages of life, from his years as a young, materially successful artist to his old age when he suffered difficulties due to lack of customers. He lost them as his art turned less commercial and more profound. These copies of several of his self-portraits show his spiritual change.

In the empty space draw your own self-portrait. As you study your face in a mirror, you must remember what you see as you take your eyes away to draw. First draw the outline shape of your face on the oval in the frame. Place the eyes on the upper horizontal lines and the mouth on the lower. Draw your nose on the vertical line, then develop the features.

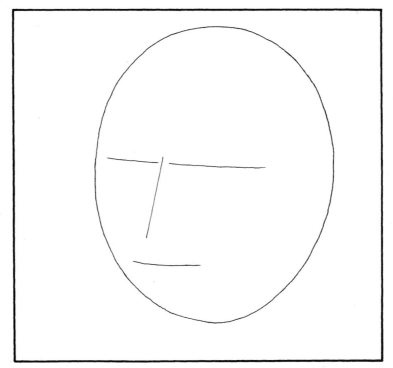

Project 61: Dutch Still Life

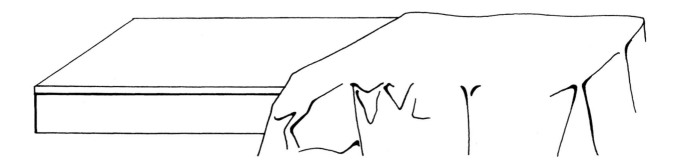

These objects were copied from several still-life paintings by Pieter Claesz (c. 1597–1661). Cut out some and carefully arrange and paste them on the tabletop. They may overlap, and you do not need to use all of the table or tablecloth. Draw a frame around your finished still-life composition.

       Studio Projects in Art History

Project 62: Still-Life Collage

A still life is a tabletop arrangement of fruit, flowers, dishware, glasses, bottles, and other items which an artist paints as realistically as possible. Find magazine advertisement pictures of such still-life objects and cut them out. Make a selection and paste them in the frame below. Arrange them carefully, for a still life cannot be a confusing collection of objects. Color any uncovered background a dark brown.

Project 63: Landscape Aerial Perspective

The dramatic seasonal changes of northern Europe provided an exciting subject for Dutch Baroque painters. Wanting to paint nature as realistically as possible, they faced a problem. They could not use Renaissance linear perspective, because nature does not have the straight lines of buildings. To give a sense of space to their landscapes, Dutch painters used *aerial perspective.* This meant giving colors a more neutral tone toward the horizon. They often introduced a road, path, or stream which wound toward a supposed vanishing point on the horizon. They alternated light and shadow bands across the canvas which acted as steps into the distance. You can see this in the small diagram of a Jacob van Ruisdael (1628/29–1682) landscape. Sketch a landscape into this frame, following the aerial-perspective suggestions noted.

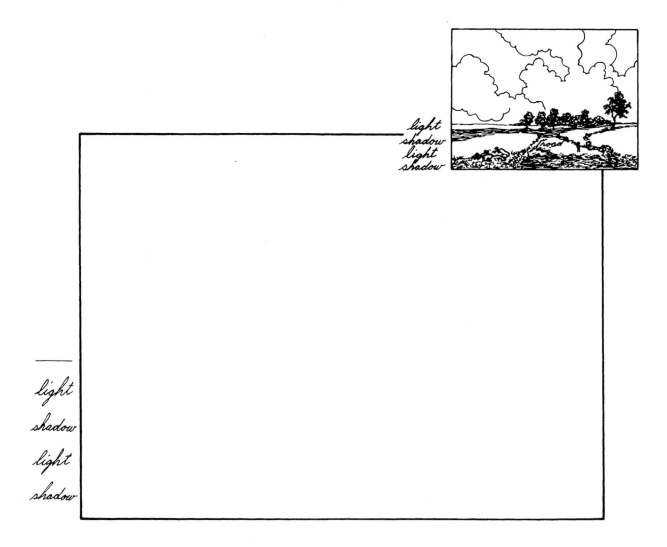

CHAPTER 18

Rococo Art

The word *Rococo* describes the late Baroque in French art and the architecture of southern German states in the first three quarters of the eighteenth century. There is something of it in English art as well, but, countered by the gruff humor of eighteenth-century English literature and the art of William Hogarth, it is less apparent.

Rococo was basically Baroque, but its excessive, decorative nature — straight lines smothered by curves, pastel colors, and themes of love and theater — seems to make it less serious. Another way to describe it, for France at least, is that Baroque was the art of King Louis XIV and Rococo was the art of King Louis XV.

A distinction can therefore be made, but it is not necessarily critical, except that Rococo has become a term for a time in art history. Its dates are slippery, for other kinds of art were produced even as Rococo ruled. The coming Neoclassical style crept into its very midst, and Fragonard, one of its most typical artists, survived long after the abdication of Rococo. And it is difficult to associate Rococo with the British colonies in America, but there it is, dressed out in blue satin suits and silver buckles, powdered wigs, lace cuffs, and the minuet.

Significant artists:

Antoine Watteau, 1684–1721

François Boucher, 1703–1770

Jean Honoré Fragonard, 1732–1806

Thomas Gainsborough, 1727–1788

Joshua Reynolds, 1723–1792

William Hogarth, 1697–1764

Rococo Art
1700–1784

In the first half of the eighteenth century, Baroque art and decoration became more extravagant, with lighter colors and less serious themes. This was especially true in France, where the aristocracy enjoyed life while failing to notice the poverty of farms and city streets. For the nobility, Rococo artists painted fanciful myths and scenes of rustic outings with pretty ladies swinging and playing games. These same lush paintings and rich architectural decorations were produced in Germany, where minor rulers tried to imitate the luxury of the French court.

Rococo Europe

Detail from *The Swing*, by Jean Honoré Fragonard

As in France, English aristocrats commissioned portraits of themselves. Although they wintered in London, they received most of their income from their large estates where they spent their summers: therefore they chose to have their portraits painted in rural settings. Portrait painters of eighteenth-century England showed less fantasy and more reserve in their art.

There also existed in England those who enjoyed satirizing the society which patronized Rococo art. Jonathan Swift ridiculed English society in *Gulliver's Travels*, as did Henry Fielding in *Tom Jones* and *Joseph Andrews*. So too did William Hogarth (1697–1764) in paintings and engravings which made sarcastic observations of the manners of the century. Rococo art, created for the idle aristocracy, was spiced by this kind of artistic good humor.

     Studio Projects in Art History

Project 64: Rococo Pleasure

Rococo painters liked to show pleasure-loving people enjoying activities such as picnicking, playing tag, swinging, dancing, and playing music in gardens filled with trees and statues. Draw a similar subject in this Rococo garden.

Student Name _____ Date _____

Project 65: English Portrait Painting

In the eighteenth century a major group of English artists painted landscapes and, more frequently, portraits. Many of the portrait painters combined the two by setting their portrait subjects in a landscape setting, painting them in an indoor studio against an imaginary landscape background.
The famous *Blue Boy* by Thomas Gainsborough (1727-1788) is one example. Using felt pens or colored pencils, create a landscape in the empty frame,
then cut out a figure from a photograph or magazine picture and paste it
into your landscape setting.

Project 66: Hogarth's Satire

Rococo art suited the tastes of society, but in his paintings and engravings William Hogarth (1697–1764) made fun of society, creating series of pictures showing how wrong-minded actions lead to downfall. Here is an outline of one series, *Marriage a la Mode*, with a detail from the second picture illustrated below.

1. A rich merchant arranges his daughter's marriage to the son of an earl, an exchange of a title for a rich dowry.

2. The new husband comes home after a night of card playing and slumps in a chair.

3. Suffering illness because of his wild life, the young husband visits a quack doctor.

4. The bored wife fills their home with useless antiques and encourages a foreign music teacher in their home.

5. The young husband is killed in a duel.

6. The young wife commits suicide.

Other series by Hogarth include *Industry and Idleness* (an industrious apprentice becomes Lord Mayor of London while his lazy friend becomes a criminal and is hanged) and *A Rake's Progress* (a young man inherits wealth, but through a life of dissipation ends up in an insane asylum).

Hogarth's art stressed the success of industrious enterprise over the excesses of a wasted life, satirizing as much as moralizing in his pictures. Think of a modern theme which could be treated in the Hogarthian manner. On the back of this sheet outline the pictures you would make to illustrate the moral of your story.

PART IV:

EARLY MODERN ART (1750–1900)

CHAPTER 19

Neoclassic Art

As a major period, the Neoclassic lasted from about 1750 until 1820. Unlike the Renaissance, which was inspired by ancient Classical art but did not copy it directly, Neoclassic artists recreated it as much as was reasonably possible. Even after it faded as a fashion, the Neoclassic period continued to influence art into the twentieth century, especially in official architecture and sculpture. Many government buildings and memorials are Neoclassic, although they were built long after the general popularity of the style had passed away.

The Neoclassic period is followed by the Romantic period (next chapter) with medieval Gothic and seventeenth-century Baroque its stylistic inspiration. Artistic debates between Neoclassic and Romantic artists enlivened newspapers throughout the nineteenth century. However, today's writers recognize the similar idea which lies at their heart: adapting the past to contemporary conditions. Therefore, most art texts now consider Neoclassic and Romantic together, acknowledging the difference in styles but sameness of spirit.

A review of Greek and Roman art supports any study of Neoclassic art. The architectural study sheet (Project 11) can be used for discovering Neoclassic features in local buildings. Neoclassic was the style (Georgian and Federal architecture) which prevailed at the time of the American Revolution: the adopted Greek and Roman words *republic, democracy, senate,* and *capital* are Neoclassic terms. Thomas Jefferson used Classical ideas when he composed the Declaration of Independence, just as he used the Neoclassic style when he designed Monticello, the Virginia State Capitol (his copy of the Maison Carrée in Nîmes), and the buildings of the University of Virginia.

Significant artists:

Jacques Louis David, 1748–1825
Pierre-Paul Prud'hon, 1758–1823
Jean-Antoine Gros, 1771–1835
Jean-Dominique Ingres, 1780–1867
Antonio Canova (sculptor), 1757–1822

Neoclassic Art
c. 1750–1820

In 1748 the buried ruins of the ancient Roman city of Pompeii were discovered. As diggers began unearthing the old statues, paintings, and buildings, the Classical style of Rome became fashionable once more. The period was therefore called *Neoclassic,* meaning "new Classic."

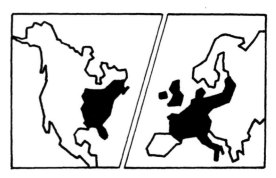

Neoclassic in Europe and America

From Russia in the east to North America in the west, architects designed buildings in the Neoclassic style. The White House is a famous example. Thomas Jefferson designed his own home, Monticello, in the Neoclassic style, and his plans for the Virginia State Capitol copied a Roman temple. All through the eastern United States and southern Canada Neoclassic buildings still survive.

After 1750 this same interest in the past caused some artists to rebel against the Rococo style with Neoclassic paintings. The new manner took over completely after Jacques Louis David (1748–1825) painted *Oath of the Horatii* in 1784.

In this painting three sons stand before Roman arches, swearing to their father that they will defend Rome or die in the attempt. With figures posed like stiff statues in formal compositions and Classical settings, Neoclassic themes were serious unlike the decorative Rococo they challenged. With the 1789 French Revolution the French king and his nobles were overthrown. So too was their Rococo art, and Neoclassic became the painting style of Western art.

Studio Projects in Art History

Project 67: History Painting

When Jacques Louis David (1748–1825) painted *Oath of the Horatii,* he used an ancient event to comment on a current situation. By depicting Roman soldiers swearing to defend the Roman republic, he was urging the people of France to struggle for their own republic. Five years before the French Revolution, it was a revolutionary painting. History painting uses a heroic theme from the past to comment on a modern issue. When in 1776 the American Benjamin West (1738–1820) painted *Penn's Treaty with the Indians,* the event had been history for almost a century.

What historical events could comment on today's issues? List some on these lines, then draw one of those events as a picture on the back of this sheet.

1. Historical event: _____

   Modern issue: _____

2. Historical event: _____

   Modern issue: _____

3. Historical event: _____

   Modern issue: _____

4. Historical event: _____

   Modern issue: _____

5. Historical event: _____

   Modern issue: _____

Project 68: Antique Ruin

Neoclassic artists found inspiration in the ruins of ancient monuments, especially those of Rome, emphasizing their ruined appearance by showing weeds, ivy, and bushes growing over broken walls and columns. This added to their antique atmosphere.

Can you think of an old building or statue near your home which is in a partly ruined condition? Sketch it in the frame below, showing how nature has begun to take over with weeds sprouting or ivy crawling over its broken brick, cracked cement, or weathered wood. What feeling does this give the picture?

Studio Projects in Art History

Project 69: Philadelphia's Roman Arch

In 1784, when news of the Treaty of Paris — officially ending the Revolutionary War — was received, celebrations were held throughout the United States. For its festivities Philadelphia commissioned painter Charles Wilson Peale (1741–1827) to erect a temporary Roman arch. Carpenters built a wooden form 35 feet high and 50 feet wide. Peale covered this with paper on which he had painted details of a classic Roman arch and scenes glorifying Washington and other war heroes. Shining through from inside, twelve hundred candles illuminated the pictures. A representation of peace (a figure holding a torch) was built for the top. On the night of the celebration, fireworks were accidentally set off atop the arch and the structure caught fire. Fireworks rockets shot into the assembled crowd; many were hurt and one man was killed.

This is a model of Peale's arch as it was described in newspapers. Cut out the two pieces, fold on the dotted lines, and assemble as shown, pasting together the head of "peace." Display the arch as an example of the Neoclassic influence in the birth of the United States.

(continued)

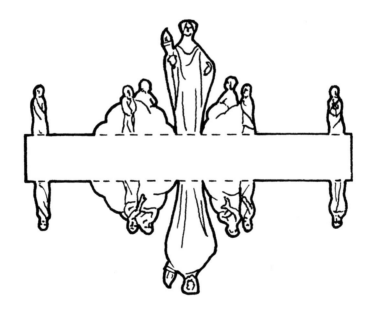

Project 69: Philadelphia's Roman Arch *(continued)*

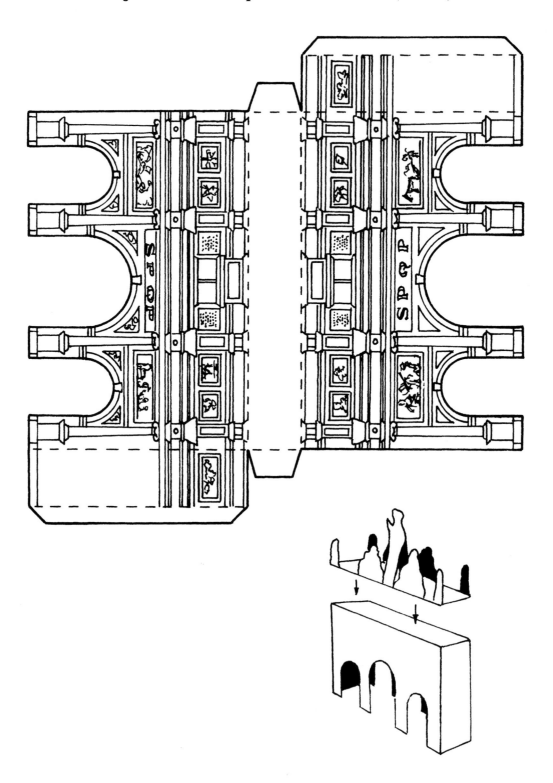

CHAPTER 20

Romantic Art

Once understood as opposites, Neoclassic and Romantic art are seen today as creations of the same cultural spirit, both calling upon the past to create imaginative art of heroic stature. Still, the two styles differ considerably, as one uses the Classical past, the other medieval Gothic and then Baroque for inspiration. Romantic neo-Gothic gave New York its Trinity Church and Saint Patrick's Cathedral, and Ottawa its principal Parliament buildings. Because most nineteenth-century North American towns still have examples of such neo-Gothic structures, Project 26 is useful for discovering Romantic-period architecture among local buildings.

Other comparisons are possible to bring meaning to this art. More than with any other style, it is reasonable to tie Romantic art to other creative arts, for most students are familiar with the literature and music of the period. The stories of Sir Walter Scott, the stories and poems of Edgar Allan Poe, and the music of Beethoven and Tchaikovsky are the most obvious examples. Romantic-period literature, music, and art entertained the nineteenth-century person as movie spectaculars entertain us today. It is no wonder that movie directors stage their films in the manner of Romantic-period art, orchestrate soundtracks with Romantic-period music, and fill their stories with all the color and excitement of Romantic-period literature. Making such comparisons and recalling the stories, poems, and music of the nineteenth century will help describe the nature of Romantic art.

Significant artists:

Francisco de Goya y Lucientes, 1746–1828
William Blake, 1757–1827
John Constable, 1776–1837
William Turner, 1775–1851
Caspar Friedrich, 1774–1840
Théodore Géricault, 1791–1824
Eugène Delacroix, 1798–1863
Jean-Baptiste Camille Corot, 1796–1875
Rosa Bonheur, 1822–1899

Romantic Art
1790–1863

Romantic art does not mean that which deals with love. Rather, it means art which is imaginative, exciting, colorful, and filled with movement: storm-tossed ships, exotic scenes, and rearing horses. Romantic art dominated much of the nineteenth century and stood in contrast to the Neoclassic style—which had little movement and rather drab color—even though Neoclassic continued in favor throughout much of the century.

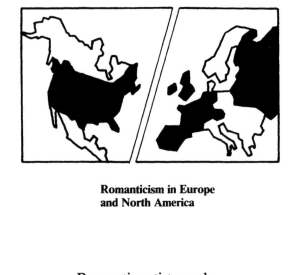

Romanticism in Europe and North America

Mounted Officer of the Imperial Guard, **by Théodore Géricault, 1812**

Romantic artists made nature appear dramatic, choosing subjects of adventure and travel and the supernatural, all for the visual excitement such subjects produced. Architects looked back to the Middle Ages and built neo-Gothic churches. Writers told stories of medieval knights and seagoing pirates. Poets dealt with nature, dreams, and death. Many of these people were as heroic as their subjects, leading romantic lives while defying tradition and society. Personalities such as the composer Beethoven, the writer Poe, and the artists Goya and Blake (as a poet), led lives as stormy as the art they created. Their music, poems, books, and pictures are as familiar today as when they were produced in the Romantic nineteenth century.

Project 70: Literature and Art

Many nineteenth-century Romantic painters enjoyed painting scenes of adventure such as travels in Africa and Asia, wild-animal hunting, and scenes of literature. They could depict such subjects with movement, excitement, and color, all in the spirit of Romantic art. In the same period some of the most popular novels of all time were written and artists painted scenes from them. *The Three Musketeers, Ivanhoe, Moby Dick,* and *Treasure Island* are just a few of the still popular Romantic-period novels.

What is your favorite nineteenth-century story? Write its title on the following line and then draw a scene from the story in the space below, giving it the excitement, movement, and color of Romantic-period art.

_____

Project 71: Goya's *Los Caprichos*

The world is a masquerade, with faces, clothes, and voices all giving a false impression. So implies Francisco Goya (1746–1828) in an etching from *Los Caprichos*. In this series of prints Goya made morbid fun of society's foolishness. In another etching from *Los Caprichos*, a child, because he is spoiled, grows up to be a silly fool. In yet another a man tells every woman he meets that he loves her. In still another of the series, a woman worships a tree, thinking it a fashionable man because good clothes have been draped on it. Choose something from modern society which you think is worthy of satire. Make fun of it with a drawing in the empty frame and title it below.

_____

_____

_____

Student Name _____   Date _____

Project 72: Blake's Illustrated Poetry

William Blake (1757–1827) was a romantic in the fullest sense of the word. Many thought him eccentric because of his mystical ideas about religion, life, and art. Because his unusual art was little appreciated in his lifetime, he and his wife lived in relative poverty, sustained by their personal spiritual happiness. In his poetry, engravings, and paintings, Blake gave vision to his metaphysical ideas. He illustrated his poetry so both poem and picture appeared in a combined composition, as in this copied example. The empty frame is the approximate size of many of his illustrated poems. Compose a poem of your own, write it in the frame, and add an illustration which supports the meaning of your poem.

Project 73: Romantic Landscape

Nature, looked at with a Romantic eye, reveals mysterious forests, awesome mountains, and dangerous seas. Important landscape painters looked at and recorded nature in nineteenth-century France, Germany, and Great Britain, while others ventured as far as the Rocky Mountains of North America. Some were content to paint only what they saw, but many emphasized nature's drama with towering mountains, beautiful sunsets, and theatrical storm clouds. Any houses or people which might appear were painted small and insignificant in the presence of nature's wonder.

Here is a simple landscape outline. Alter it, add to it, and color it to bring out the drama of nature.

CHAPTER 21

Realist Art

In the mid-nineteenth century Gustave Courbet disclaimed the artificialities of Neoclassic and Romantic art and took for himself the term *Realism*. Although he did paint in a realistic style, even doing still lifes as had earlier artists, it was subject rather than style which he emphasized as realistic. He depicted ordinary people as they really lived: workers sweating, a funeral, courtesans picnicking, unattractive people in unattractive activities. There were heavy political overtones to Courbet's art in an era when early socialism concerned itself with the same constituency that appeared in Courbet's paintings.

As a movement, Courbet's was almost a solo performance. Yet, many others responding to the social problems of the time can be considered Realists — Daumier, certain English painters, and Millet, who "romanticized" his peasant subjects. After Courbet, Manet considered himself a Realist and was an Impressionist only by association.

Another art drops unconsciously into this category. It is photography, for these were its pioneer years. Many early photographers tried to be "arty" by staging studio set-ups fashioned after Neoclassic and Romantic paintings. Today they are fun to see as period pieces, serious work turned comic. An exception is the work of photographers such as Matthew Brady (c. 1823–1896), who, in the Courbet tradition, show us the way it really was.

Realism should be considered in its historical context, for it speaks of the mid-nineteenth century in ways in which academic Neoclassicism and Romantic art did not. Leaving behind country lanes for a hard look at city streets and alleys, Realist artists inform us about the nineteenth century in the way Charles Dickens does with his novels.

This chapter considers labor as a subject and examines the art of Daumier. Victorian photography and narrative painting, a minor but entertaining side of nineteenth-century art, contribute two more projects.

Significant artists:

Jean François Millet, 1814–1875   Ford Madox Brown, 1821–1893
Honoré Daumier, 1808–1879   Winslow Homer, 1836–1910
Gustave Courbet, 1819–1877   Thomas Eakins, 1844–1916

Student Name _____ Date _____

Realist Art
1830–1874

The last two thirds of the nineteenth century have been called the Victorian era, after Great Britain's ruling Queen Victoria. Neoclassic and Romantic painting continued throughout the period, but some artists disliked it. They felt that neither style showed life as it was really lived. Some dubbed themselves Realists. Although they did paint in a realistic

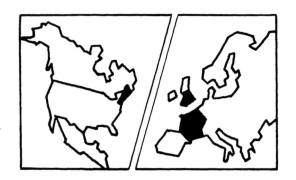

**Major Realist art in
Europe and North America**

style, the realism they were interested in was a matter of subject rather than style. They painted real life: everyday problems, work, everyone's joys and tragedies. In France the movement was most noticeable. Other countries had Realists, too. In the United States Winslow Homer (1836–1910) of New England and Thomas Eakins (1844–1916) of Philadelphia stand out.

**Detail from *The Stone Breakers*
by Gustave Courbet, 1849**

It surprises us today, but a century ago Realist art was radical and controversial. It was a threat not only to established painters, but a threat to the upper classes which bought art, for it made workers and the poor, such as a ragged boy carrying rocks in Gustave Courbet's (1819–1877) *The Stone Breakers*, important enough for fine art. Charles Dickens was doing the same in his novels.

Realist art could be very political. Honoré Daumier (1808–1879) was imprisoned for six months due to one of his drawings. Courbet was nearly executed for his part in the Paris Commune of 1870. Those political events are largely forgotten today. But Realist art remains to show us what life was like a century ago as the Industrial Revolution got up to full steam and cities began their first growth explosions.

Project 74: Work Subjects

Nineteenth-century Realist artists felt that ordinary labor was a fit subject for art. Jean François Millet (1814–1875) painted poor peasants at work in the fields of France. Gustave Courbet (1819–1877) depicted a construction worker breaking stones by hand. Ford Madox Brown (1821–1893) created a large painting, entitled *Work*, which shows laborers digging a tunnel amidst a collection of other activities. Some Realists painted the factories and mills which changed the nineteenth-century landscape. They depicted their workers as heroic, even when their labor was backbreaking, and their factories glowed dramatically with blast furnaces lighting up night skies.

What work, typical of your community, would be a fit subject for art and would show something of how people spend their working day? Write the name of such work on the line below, then describe how it could be given a heroic appearance. Then draw, paint, or photograph the subject, showing the dignity and heroism of ordinary work.

_____

kind of work

_____

_____

_____

_____

Project 75: Daumier's Faces

For over forty years Honoré Daumier's (1808–1879) drawings appeared in French newspapers, showing life as it was in Paris, often with humorous social and political comment. In his day political drawings were frequently censured, and Daumier was once jailed for one of his. The faces on this page are copied from a series of prominent political figures Daumier drew in 1831. He exaggerated their features for recognition and humor. Select photographs of four individuals, either politicians (look in newspaper) or your friends. In the empty frames, draw their faces, exaggerating the features.

Masques de 1831

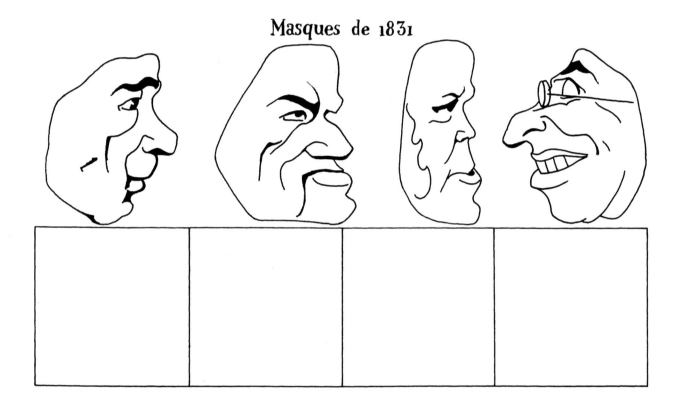

Project 76: Narrative Painting

Genre painting, pictures which depict ordinary people in real-life situations, flourished in the nineteenth century. The literary interest of the nineteenth century affected it, for many genre paintings of the period tell a story. Look at *Fidelity* by Briton Rivière (1840–1920) copied here. The window tells you this is a prison scene with the prisoner in deep despair. He must sleep on the straw on the floor. The gallows graffiti scratched on the wall lets you know he will die, with only his faithful dog left with him (hence the title) in his last days. Such storytelling art is called *narrative painting.*

Choose one of the following titles of other nineteenth-century narrative paintings and draw or describe in the empty frame the way you would visually tell the story. *The Tired Seamstress; The Lost Path; Not Forgotten; The Last Evening; Trouble; An Anxious Hour; The First Cloud; The Soldier's Farewell; The Outcast; The Broken Window; The Escape; St. Valentine's Morning.*

Project 77: Victorian Photo Frame

In the early days of photography in the middle of the nineteenth century there was no such thing as an instant snapshot, for long exposures were needed to capture an image. People wanting a photo portrait sat in a studio just as they might sit for a

painted portrait. They framed their photo portraits with all the care of paintings. They even framed small studio portraits as elaborately as large photographs. You can make a nineteenth-century photo frame for one of your photo portraits.

1. Select an appropriate photograph.

2. Cut a thick piece of cardboard the size of the photo.

3. Glue the photo to the cardboard backing.

4. Cut a piece of gold foil the size of the photo. Cut an oval hole in the foil and score a decorative design with a blunt point.

5. Cut a second, gold-foil frame with an opening ⅛″ smaller than the photo, and side tabs extending ½″ beyond the photo edge. Score a decorative design in this inner frame if you wish.

6. Lay the oval frame over the photo and (optional) cover with a piece of thin, clear plastic cut to size.

7. Lay the outer foil frame over the photo package and bend the tabs behind to hold all in place.

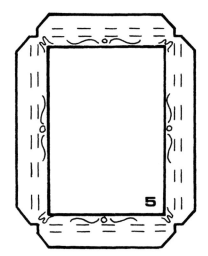

CHAPTER 22

Impressionism

Impressionism is probably the most popular historical art style and is chronologically important as the movement from which sprouted twentieth-century art. To be appreciated and understood it needs to be seen, either as museum originals or good book reproductions. It is difficult to construct an exercise which offers the Impressionist experience; however, Project 78 of this chapter does attempt to imitate Impressionism with felt pens. The other exercises treat other aspects of Impressionist art. Included is an exercise in Pointillism (perhaps more properly placed in the following chapter, but as an extension of Impressionist technique it is included here).

The approach taken by the American James Whistler was akin to the art of Manet and, like the Frenchman, Whistler became more Impressionistic in his later work. Project 78 borrows the portrait of his mother to demonstrate his sense of composition. A diagram of Whistler's composition which you will need for Project 78 is drawn here.

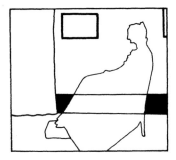

Because of its special way of looking at nature and the anti-establishment attitudes of those associated with it, Impressionism looks ahead to modern art. Yet, it evolved out of the art environment of the nineteenth century — Romantic landscape painting and Realism. The Impressionists felt they were of the Realist tradition of Courbet and Manet, for they dealt with similar subjects, rendering them, in their view, in a realistic, scientific manner. Yet for all these observations, it is the pleasure we receive from Impressionist painting which is the most important consideration.

Significant artists:

Édouard Manet, 1832–1883
James McNeill Whistler, 1834–1903
Claude Monet, 1840–1926
Berthe Morisot, 1841–1895
Mary Cassatt, 1845–1926
Camille Pissarro, 1830–1903
Alfred Sisley, 1839–1899

Pierre Auguste Renoir, 1841–1919
Edgar Degas, 1834–1917

Pointillists

Georges Seurat, 1859–1891
Paul Signac, 1863–1935

Impressionism
1874–1886

The Impressionists began in the tradition of Realist art, depicting ordinary people (usually enjoying themselves) picnicking, dancing, boating, or on outings in the landscapes of northern France. However, it is the way they painted, and not the subject matter, which is important to Impressionism.

France

**Diagram of *Impression, Sunrise*
by Claude Monet**

Adapting some of the science of optics researched in the nineteenth century, the Impressionists understood that when we look at something we see not the object itself, but light reflected from it. Our eyes perceive the object as many small spots of color of varying shades and tones, not as a solid-color shape. To capture this optical sensation, they worked on small canvases set up outdoors, painting with small color strokes. Working quickly before the sun shifted to any great degree, they were able to produce a feeling of spontaneity rather than posed studio effects. What they achieved were bright paintings with colors shimmering like the reflection of sunlight on the surface of water. It became one of the most popular kinds of painting ever created.

The public first scorned the Impressionists when they exhibited together in 1874. By the time of their last exhibition in 1886, Impressionism had spread well beyond the borders of France. It continued to be an important art technique, but will always be associated with France in the last quarter of the nineteenth century.

Project 78: Arranging Whistler's Mother

James McNeill Whistler's (1834–1903) painting of his mother is properly titled *Arrangement in Black and Gray: The Artist's Mother*. The title tells you the artist's interest was less in portraying his mother and more in creating an arrangement of flat shapes.

At the bottom of the next page sits his mother. Also pictured in this exercise are doorway coverings, partial and whole picture frames, and black baseboards. Select some of compatible shape and arrange them within the picture. Pieces can overlap. How close do you come to Whistler's original composition?

(continued)

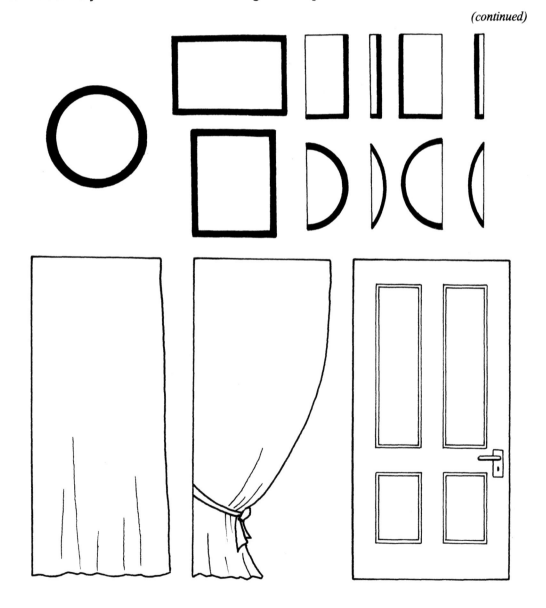

Project 78: Arranging Whistler's Mother *(continued)*

Project 79: Impressionist Technique

The Impressionists built up their paintings with small strokes of their brushes, perceiving each stroke as a reflection of some color: a yellow stroke, a red stroke, and so on. The artist who practiced Impressionism in the strictest manner was Claude Monet (1840–1926). Lightly sketched here is his painting *The River Seine at Argenteuil.*

1. Color the picture using broad-tipped felt pens, applying color in short strokes.

2. Don't color an area in solid color. Instead, use different colors next to one another: light green, dark green, blue, and yellow in the trees, for example.

3. Consider carefully sunlit areas and shade, such as the shadow below the bridge, and reflections in the water.

4. Don't concentrate on a single part of the picture: move about, bringing the whole drawing to a conclusion as a complete composition.

Project 80: Degas' Dancers

Although Edgar Degas (1834–1917) exhibited with the Impressionists and used some of their theories, he was not a strict Impressionist because he generally painted interiors with people rather than outdoor landscapes. This meant his style had to be more linear and could not be reduced to short brush strokes. One of his favorite subjects was ballet dancers. Most often he painted them at practice or warming up for a dance, stretching in an extreme pose such as the dancer pictured here. Imagine some of the unusual moves you make, or see your friends make, when dancing. Draw such a dance position in this frame.

Project 81: Pointillist Technique

A few French painters called Neo-Impressionists took Impressionism one step further by reducing brush strokes to mere dots, calling their method *Pointillism.* When painting a color area, a green bush for example, they painted dots of not only shades of green, but also blue and yellow, which together appear green; red and yellow with oranges; and blue and red with purples. They also included contrasting dots, such as red with green, to give the color area more vibrancy. The dots did not always touch one another; some white canvas might be left around them.

Use this description of Pointillism to color this diagram of a detail from Georges Seurat's (1859–1891) *Sunday Afternoon on the Grande Jatte,* making color dots with the tips of fine-point felt pens.

         Studio Projects in Art History

CHAPTER 23

Post-Impressionism

Roger Fry coined the term *Post-Impressionism* for the 1910 art exhibition he arranged in London. Although it included works by Vlaminck, Rouault, Picasso, and other living painters, the emphasis was on Cézanne, Van Gogh, and Gauguin. Therefore, the name of the exhibit, Post-Impressionism, stuck to them, as well as to the Pointillists and Toulouse-Lautrec. The title is convenient. It includes those artists who came out of Impressionism to develop their own manner and make an impact on twentieth-century developments.

The exercises included here emphasize the principal contributions of the artists they describe: Cézanne's sense of painting structure, Van Gogh's emphasis on emotional expression, and Gauguin's stress of color for its own sake. Not that their work does not offer much more, but these are keys to their art. Two additional projects introduce Toulouse-Lautrec's poster art and the concept of Art Nouveau.

Due to its place in cultural time, most French art of the 1890s, including Art Nouveau, can be described as Post-Impressionist. However, Art Nouveau was certainly not confined to France. Inspired in part by the sinuous lines and shapes found in the art of Gauguin and Toulouse-Lautrec, it was popular enough to become fashionable. Art Nouveau spread throughout Europe, but, in a little more than a decade, faded as all fashions do.

The most substantial Post-Impressionist art was that of Cézanne, Gauguin, and Van Gogh, not only because of its continued aesthetic value, but for pointing the way into the twentieth century. If Post-Impressionist on the one hand, it is pre-Modern on the other.

Significant artists:

Paul Cézanne, 1839–1906
Paul Gauguin, 1848–1903
Vincent van Gogh, 1853–1890
Henri de Toulouse-Lautrec, 1864–1901

Art Nouveau

Aubrey Beardsley, 1872–1898
Gustav Klimt, 1862–1918

France

Post-Impressionism
1886–1905

Impressionism, the breaking up of color areas into small strokes of paint, had its limitations. Solid objects and hard lines appeared to blur into misty shapes. Artists wishing to render subjects more solidly, or to depict figures and structures, felt the need to depart from strict Impressionism.

Henri de Toulouse-Lautrec (1864–1901) used the bright colors of Impressionism with a strong linear style to paint personalities of Paris nightlife. Paul Cézanne (1839–1906) emphasized solidity by building up a painting until it was something new, yet based upon a recognizable subject. Paul Gauguin (1848–1903) painted in remote places such as rural Brittany in France and then in the South Pacific, exploring color simply for the pleasure it gave. Vincent van Gogh (1853–1890) used colors and forms for the emotional impact they could produce.

A tree can be used to compare their different approaches. A Cézanne tree (1) has a feeling of solid form. A Gauguin tree (2) presents a bright color shape of delightful pattern. A Van Gogh tree (3) seems alive with emotional energy.

1   2   3

Some of their art had an immediate impact. The curving lines and shapes in the art of Gauguin and Toulouse-Lautrec helped inspire Art Nouveau, meaning *new art*. Art Nouveau, rich in original curvilinear forms and lines, was used in architecture, furniture design, and graphic art. Because of its very fashionable nature it did not last. Yet the art of the Post-Impressionist painters, especially that of Cézanne, Gauguin, and Van Gogh, became major influences on twentieth-century art.

Project 82: Cézanne Still Life

Still-life paintings show how Paul Cézanne (1839–1906) viewed his art and contributed ideas which would be important in the coming twentieth century. First he arranged objects on a table. When he painted such a still-life setup, he arranged further by changing the objects on the canvas: stretching the side of a bottle, flattening fruit shapes, twisting a glass so it was in harmony with the shape of an adjacent apple, turning a rumpled tablecloth into a flat pattern, all for the sake of composition. His painting was no longer an accurate pictorial record of the objects on the table, but something new and unique in itself. Alter this still-life diagram with darker lines in the same manner to make a more satisfactory composition. Then color your still life, using the same good sense of composition.

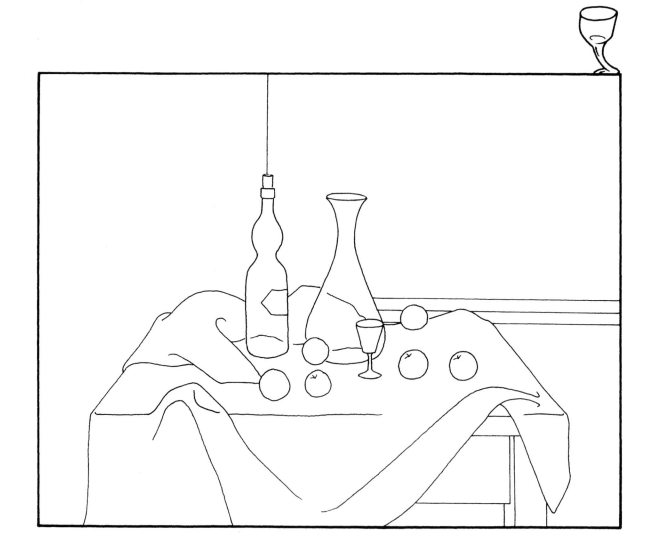

 Studio Projects in Art History

Project 83: Gauguin's Paradise

Paul Gauguin (1848–1903) was a successful businessman with a wife and children when he became fascinated with art. His interest grew until he gave up his business to live solely as a painter. Disliking a city environment, he left Paris for Brittany on the French coast to paint rural peasant life. Yet that was not far enough from European civilization for Gauguin, so he sailed to Tahiti in the South Pacific. There he created paintings rich in the color of the islands, flattening the images of Pacific landscapes to enhance that color.

If you wanted to escape modern life, where would you go? Decide upon a place, then look for photographs of it in magazines, books, or travel brochures. Select a suitable photograph and let it inspire a color drawing in this frame. Exaggerate and even change colors to give something of the feeling of the environment as you imagine it.

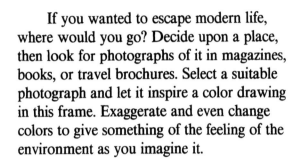

Project 84: Van Gogh's Letters

In his many letters to his brother, Vincent van Gogh (1853–1890) often mentioned paintings he was working on, emphasizing the emotions he was trying to express. Below are some excerpts from those letters. Select one and on the back of this sheet describe or sketch with colored pens or pencils your interpretation of what he was trying to do.

In my picture of the *Night Café* I have tried to express the idea that it is a place where one can ruin one's self. Everywhere there is a clash and contrast of the most alien reds and greens in the empty, dreary room.

Meanwhile I have a portrait of Dr. Gachet with the heartbroken expression of our time.

I have tried to emphasize that these people (*The Potato Eaters*), eating their potatoes in the lamplight, have dug the earth with the same hands they put in the dish and, therefore, it tells of manual labor and how they have honestly earned their food.

At the moment I am working on some blossoming plum trees, yellowish white with thousands of black branches.

I am thinking of decorating my studio with pictures of sunflowers; a decoration in which chrome yellow shall blaze forth against various backgrounds of blue, the kind of effect which Gothic stained-glass windows give.

Here is a description of the canvas . . . on the right a gray terrace and a side wall of the house. Some deflowered rose bushes, on the left a park . . . the earth burnt by the sun, covered with fallen pine needles.

Here is the sketch, simply my bedroom, only here color is to do everything . . . to be suggestive of rest or of sleep. The walls are pale violet. The floor is of red tiles. The wood of the bed and the chairs are the yellow of fresh butter, the sheets and pillows are a very light greenish lemon. The coverlet is scarlet. The window green. The washstand orange, the basin blue. The doors lilac.

Project 85: Toulouse-Lautrec Poster

   Henri de Toulouse-Lautrec (1864–1901) painted many pictures of Paris night-life, using the strong colors introduced by the Impressionists, the sturdy line of Degas, and the flat shapes of Japanese prints popular at the end of the nineteenth century. Toulouse-Lautrec also designed posters advertising nightclub and cabaret entertainments. Because of his talent, he made poster art a fine art. In the examples copied here you can see the flat shapes, imagine the bright colors, and enjoy the strong, swinging line of the main figures.

   Let these examples of Toulouse-Lautrec's art influence a poster for some school activity. On a sheet of paper or poster board, design the letters along with the picture material.

Project 86: Art Nouveau Design

Although they were not Art Nouveau artists, the lines and shapes in many paintings of Toulouse-Lautrec and Gauguin inspired Art Nouveau design. Art Nouveau shapes and lines curve gently, swell and grow thin as if they are growing like plants. Designers used Art Nouveau lines and shapes for furniture and lamps, architectural decoration, letter shapes, and fabric patterns. Below are typical Art Nouveau plant shapes. In the same style create an Art Nouveau design of your own in the empty space.

PART V:

MODERN ART
(TWENTIETH CENTURY)

CHAPTER 24

Fauve Art and Cubism

Although it has been almost ninety years since Fauve art first appeared, it seems thoroughly "modern." When it did appear at the Autumn Salon of 1905, it was the most "modern" feature of the new century, a time when royalty still dominated Europe and floor-length skirts and huge hats were the feminine fashion. Put into its historical context, Fauve art is the most modern art ever created.

Experimentation was the key word for Fauves—experimenting to produce something new, paintings which were new in themselves and not an impression or copy of something seen or experienced. The Fauves looked at color for its own sake, an approach which Gauguin had preached.

Students should learn how to treat color for what it can offer—to seek new combinations and shades and use them for expressive results. It means discovering the underlying pattern of objects and arranging shapes to produce different feelings. It is going to the heart of creativity to produce something new with such basic ingredients as color and pattern.

Two years after the 1905 introduction of the Fauves, Picasso and Braque began their Cubist experiments. Three quarters of a century later Cubism can still be difficult to understand, because the Cubists in their most theoretical art were not concerned with emotions or message. So what was it all about? It was the creation of something new, complete in itself, even though it usually began with an actual object in view. The painting itself became an object, and the subject slipped into irrelevance. Although in time the Cubists became interested in color, their earliest works, inspired by the structural approach of Cézanne, were built upon solid shapes; therefore, light and dark tones rather than color. Cubist projects in this chapter stress the analytical approach to creativity, which may offer a new insight into art for many students.

Significant artists:

Fauve artists:	**Cubist artists:**
Henri Matisse, 1869–1954	Pablo Picasso, 1881–1973
Maurice de Vlaminck, 1876–1958	Georges Braque, 1882–1963
André Derain, 1880–1954	Juan Gris, 1887–1927
Raoul Dufy, 1877–1953	Fernand Léger, 1881–1955

Fauve Art and Cubism
1905 and 1907

France

The first shock of modern art appeared at the Paris Autumn Salon of 1905 with works by Henri Matisse (1869–1954), André Derain (1880–1954), and others. A newspaper critic called them the *Fauves,* French for "wild beasts," because of the radical nature of their art. Even when these artists went their separate ways, the name stuck. The most unifying factor in the work of the Fauves was experimentation with color and pattern. The leading Fauve was Matisse, whose aim was to create paintings in which color, line, and composition expressed feelings such as joy, harmony, or rhythm. This detail, copied from the Matisse painting *The Dance,* uses line to give the sense of swinging rhythm, the glide and sway of dance music.

**Detail from *The Dance,*
by Henri Matisse**

In 1907 Pablo Picasso (1881–1973) created *Les Demoiselles d'Avignon,* a painting completely different in approach from other modern works. Together with Georges Braque (1882–1963), Picasso was partly inspired by Cézanne's method of arranging subjects to emphasize their solidity. The geometric style of African sculpture also influenced their ideas. The term *Cubism* was applied to their approach because they seemed to reduce objects to geometric shapes. A better description is that Picasso and Braque took their subjects apart and put them back together in new ways, distorting shapes, rearranging parts, reconstructing the subject so it became something totally new and different. Like Fauve art, Cubism involved visual experimentation; the Cubists experimented with shape and forms, the Fauves with color, line, and pattern.

Project 87: Harmonious Forms

These six drawings duplicate photographs made over the two-month period of the development of Henri Matisse's (1869–1954) *Lady in Blue*. Beginning with a seated woman as the subject, Matisse reworked the forms to bring the shapes and curves into harmony with one another until he had created a painting unique in itself, not a record of the original subject.

Sketch a snapshot or magazine photograph in frame 1. Redraw it in frame 2, altering the shapes into a flat pattern. Draw it a final time in frame 3, harmonizing the shapes and curves.

1

2

3

       Studio Projects in Art History

Project 88: Matisse and Color

Color for pleasure and composition was a major motivation in the art of Henri Matisse (1869–1954). That is obvious when you read the titles of some of his paintings, such as *Plum Tree on Green Background, Harmony in Red, Still Life with Red Fish* and *The Green Sideboard*. Matisse painted flat shapes in order to apply colors at their strongest, then chose and arranged those colors in a harmonious way. Here is a diagram of Matisse's *Lady in Blue*, accompanied by the color scheme of the painting. You, however, are to select other colors, carefully consider their arrangement, and color this picture to produce a harmonious composition.

Color Plan of
Lady in Blue

b - greenish blue
y - yellow
r - red
w - white
bk - black
dress - greenish blue
hands, face - pink
hair, necklace - orange
beads - black & white

158   *Studio Projects in Art History*

Project 89: Matisse Cut-outs

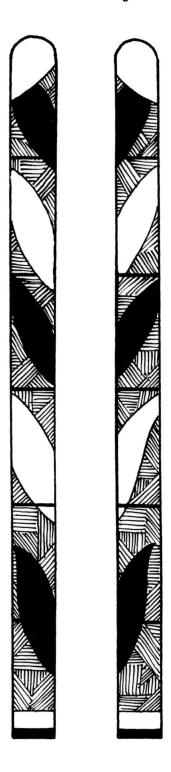

Near the end of his life Henri Matisse (1869–1954) suffered a serious illness which left him bedridden. Unable to paint, he made compositions by cutting paper which assistants had colored, then pasting them in various arrangements. Some of these compositions were remade in tile or stained glass, such as the yellow, blue, and green *Tree of Life* on the left, now in a French church. The other example, on the next page, copies a section of *The Swimming Pool,* which is tan, white, and blue.

1. Tape stiff paper to a work surface.

2. Brush clear water over the paper.

3. Let the water soak in until no puddles remain.

4. Mix a tempera color to the thickness of cream.

5. Brush the color evenly over the damp paper.

(continued)

     Studio Projects in Art History

Project 89: Matisse Cut-outs *(continued)*

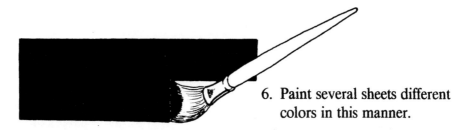

6. Paint several sheets different
   colors in this manner.

7. Cut shapes from the colored paper.

8. Experiment with different shapes and color combinations
   on a colored background.

9. Decide on a composition and paste in place.

Project 90: Cubist Composition

The earliest Cubist art analyzed the geometric shapes of objects; an orange is a sphere, a box is a cube. However, Cubist subjects were much more complex. The upper drawing copies Georges Braque's (1882–1963) *Houses in L'Estaque* in which he eliminated details, such as windows, to render the buildings as solid blocks, rearranging them in a logical composition. Color was not important in early Cubist paintings. Grays, browns, yellow ochres, and greens were used to render three-dimensional forms rather than flat patterns.

Use the lower sketch of houses, or another picture of your choosing, as a basis for a Cubist construction in the empty frame.

Project 91: Cubist Collage

The Cubists invented the art of collage, in which they pasted scraps of paper (wrapping paper, theater tickets, magazine and newspaper rippings, candy wrappers, etc.) on a sheet of paper. They did not cover the entire space on which they pasted the paper pieces. Sometimes they added drawn lines to complete the Cubist design, at all times paying attention to the visually logical arrangement of the pieces. Make your Cubist collage in the space below.

1. Collect various kinds of scrap paper.

2. Select pieces that go well together in color and design.

3. Draw a frame around the empty space below.

4. Arrange and rearrange the selected scraps until you have made an arrangement you like.

5. Paste the scraps in the frame in that arrangement.

6. Draw lines into the collage design if you wish.

CHAPTER 25

Neo-Plasticism and Suprematism

In some ways, completely abstract painting is more comprehensible than early Cubism, because by removing all subject matter a painting is understood as something unique in itself. The term *abstract*, with its many possible interpretations, is less preferable than the terms *nonobjective* or *nonrepresentational*, which more aptly describe the lack of any subject in this sort of painting.

Such is the art of this chapter on Suprematism and Neo-Plasticism. Both movements developed out of Cubism, for as Picasso and Braque manipulated geometric shapes, they moved toward nonobjective painting. Neither artist ever lost sight of his subject, however. It was left for the Suprematist Kasimir Malevich in Russia to do this in 1913. In the same year another Russian, Wassily Kandinsky, did the same in Munich, but his nonobjective art grew out of Expressionism, the theme of the following chapter. In the same World War I decade, Dutch artists moved from Cubism to nonobjective art in a movement described by Mondrian as Neo-Plasticism.

In their search for "pure" art, both movements were theoretical and analytical. It is the analytical which is stressed in this chapter. In Project 93, students are asked to arrange colors in two Mondrian paintings. It is not important that they reach his conclusion. They might even try colors other than Mondrian's primary colors for their exercise. For reference, the illustration below shows Mondrian's color arrangement.

> *Significant artists:*
>
> Kasimir Malevich, 1878–1935
> Piet Mondrian, 1872–1944
> Theo van Doesburg, 1883–1931

Color key to Mondrian solutions:
   R - red
   B - blue
   Y - yellow

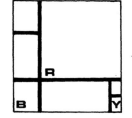
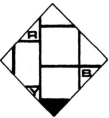

Neo-Plasticism and Suprematism
1913 and 1920

The Fauves and Cubists generally retained something of a subject in their paintings. They seldom went so far as to produce a completely nonobjective painting. *Nonobjective* is a term preferred over the word *abstract* for describing art which consists only of lines, shapes, and colors, with no recognizable object present. The illustration here is an example of a nonobjective drawing.

Holland and Russia

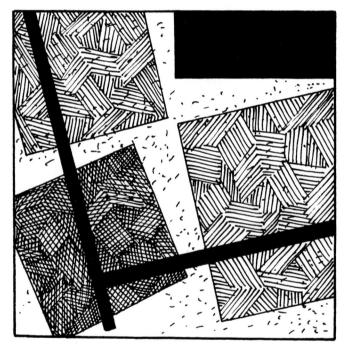

One of the first nonobjective painters was the Russian Kasimir Malevich (1878–1935). By 1913 he was painting only flat geometric shapes of bright colors. Eventually he even eliminated color from his art. In 1913 he did a picture with two black squares on a white background. Several years later he painted a tilted white square on a white background, the two whites differing only slightly in shade and texture. Malevich called his art *Suprematism* and influenced many artists in Russia in the years before 1922.

The twentieth century's most familiar nonobjective painter is Piet Mondrian, (1872–1944) who, with other Dutch painters, formed a movement which Mondrian first called *Neo-Plasticism* in 1920. It has also carried the title *De Stijl*, the name of a Dutch art magazine. The illustration copied on this page is by Theo van Doesburg (1883–1931), the most theoretical of the Dutch Neo-Plasticists.

 Studio Projects in Art History

Project 92: To Abstraction

Like most early painters of nonobjective (abstract) art, Piet Mondrian
(1872–1944) first painted real objects, such as trees (1). In time Mondrian's tree
became more abstract (2). Then he painted only lines and shapes (3), vaguely recalling
his tree paintings. Cover copies 2 and 3, and in the top frame draw your abstract
impression of the tree. Follow that with a nonobjective picture based on your drawing.

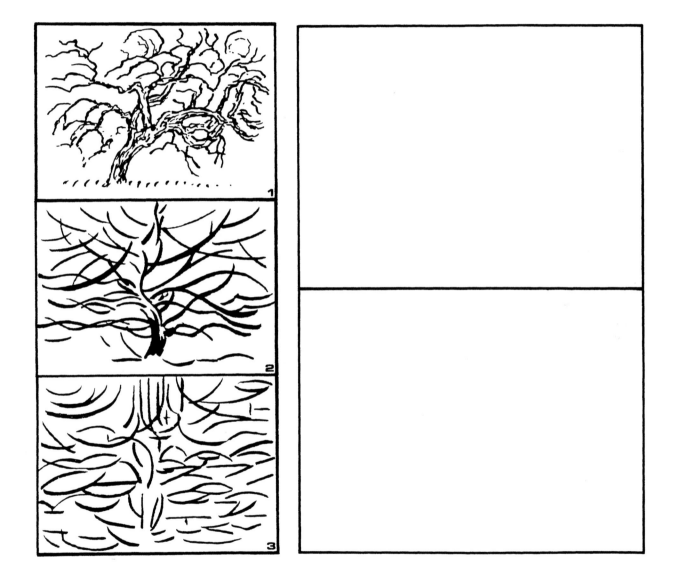

Project 93: Mondrian's Colors

Piet Mondrian (1872–1944) sought to create "pure" art, paintings which projected no story, no emotion, no message. Pursuing this goal, he reduced his paintings to the most basic elements: straight lines and right angles and the primary colors of red, blue, and yellow plus white and black. These he carefully arranged in the most balanced composition in order not to disturb a painting by any sense of unbalance.

Below are copies of two Mondrian paintings without their color. *Composition with Red, Blue and Yellow,* on the left, has those three colors plus white in some spaces. *Composition in Red, Yellow and Blue,* on the right, has black and white spaces as well as spaces with the three primaries. Think carefully about each painting and then color in the spaces in the way you think Mondrian might have done it. Write on the back of this sheet your reasons for arranging the colors as you did.

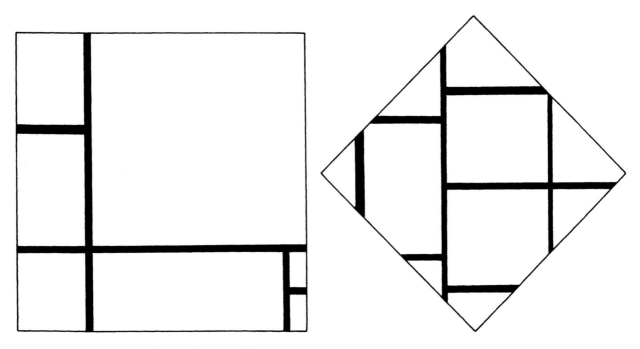

Composition with Red, Blue and Yellow   *Composition in Red, Yellow and Blue*

         Studio Projects in Art History

Project 94: Suprematist Composition

The Russian Kasimir Malevich (1878–1935) first painted as a Cubist, but his art became more and more abstract as he tried to achieve "the supremacy of pure feeling or perception." From his statement came the term *Suprematist* for his art. By then no object appeared in his paintings, only geometric shapes of various colors. In 1918 Malevich painted *Suprematist Composition: White on White*, a tilted white square on a white square background. They could only be distinguished from one another because each was an off-white of a different tone.

Decide on a *single* color for your Suprematist composition, then find that color in a felt-tipped pen, a ball-point pen, a crayon, and a colored pencil. In the empty space below, draw and color an arrangement of geometric shapes with one or more of these utensils, then color in the background with another. Although the color remains the same, the shapes and background can be distinguished by the different coloring utensils you used.

CHAPTER 26

Expressionism

A great number of twentieth-century artists could be described as expressionists — the Frenchman Georges Rouault and the Englishman Francis Bacon, for example. The same is true of earlier artists. Michelangelo, El Greco, and Grünewald could be and have been described as expressionist because of the strong emotions expressed in their art. Expressionism, emotional art loaded with message, is a state of mind rather than an art style.

Van Gogh was the artistic father of twentieth-century Expressionism. But as a specific modern movement it is generally confined to Germany in the first third of the century, hence the term *German Expressionism.* It is not difficult to understand why. Militarism, economic depression, rampant inflation, dictatorship, being the loser in two world wars, and the climactic horror of the Nazi era all are sufficient reasons for producing an artistic outlook based on emotions and message. The German experience of the first half of this century should be considered when examining twentieth-century Expressionist art.

Do students feel strongly about any current events? Is all well with their world, or do they see pockets of injustice and misery? It takes a strong commitment to make an expressionist, either artist, writer, or missionary. Let them think about issues and conditions and examine how the German Expressionists dealt with their commitments, not in a direct propagandist manner or as political cartoonists, but as painters with color and line delivering messages on their views of the human condition.

To help students express their own concerns, one project deals with expressive lines, another with expressive color, and a third with expressive composition. The other projects deal with Expressionist themes. The Abstract Expressionism of Kandinsky is treated in Chapter 28; Paul Klee of the Blue Rider group is discussed in Chapter 27.

Significant artists:	Die Brücke	Der Blaue Reiter
Edvard Munch, 1863–1944	Ernst Ludwig Kirchner, 1880–1938	Wassily Kandinsky, 1866–1944
Käthe Kollwitz, 1867–1945		Franz Marc, 1880–1916
Oskar Kokoschka, 1886–1980	Max Pechstein, 1881–1955	August Macke, 1887–1914
Max Beckmann, 1884–1950	Otto Mueller, 1874–1930	Paul Klee, 1879–1940

Germany

Expressionism
1905 and 1913

In the year of the first Fauve exhibition, 1905, several German artists banded together in a group called *Die Brücke*, meaning "The Bridge." They hoped to serve as a bridge to unite all new German art. The approach of most German artists in the early decades of the century was to express their relationship to society. This led to intense artistic message and emotion in their art, giving them the name *Expressionists*.

Even before 1905 the Norwegian artist Edvard Munch (1863–1944) and the German Käthe Kollwitz (1867–1945) — one of her drawings is copied here at left — were creating Expressionist art in Berlin. Many German Expressionists chose to paint as independents instead of associating in a group. The 1913 Munich group, *Der Blaue Reiter* ("The Blue Rider"), modified their Expressionism, stressing color and composition rather than emotions.

When you look at Expressionist art, you might be shocked by the harsh colors and rugged composition. Expressionist artists often aimed to shock in order to make you think, to disturb you, to make you react to the emotions of their art. Käthe Kollwitz depicted starvation and poverty. Max Beckmann (1884–1950) showed the horrid side of modern civilization. Ernst Ludwig Kirchner (1880–1938) rendered the emptiness of sophisticated urban life. To be an Expressionist is to feel strongly about something and then express your message with color, line, and composition.

       Studio Projects in Art History

Student Name _____   Date _____

Project 95: Expressive Lines

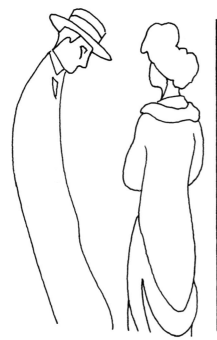

Lines can express feelings. Smoothly curving lines suggest ease and quiet, as in August Macke's (1887–1914) *Promenade*. Lines with sharp angles and jagged, abrupt turns, as in Max Pechstein's (1881–1955) *The Tempter*, express action or stress. Paste an interesting newspaper photograph in the small frame, then sketch it in the larger frame using lines which express the feelings of the photograph.

(continued)

         Studio Projects in Art History

Project 95: Expressive Lines *(continued)*

Project 96: Color Expression

Expressionists boldly used color to emphasize human feelings and personality. Cool colors such as greens and blues produce a sense of calm. Warmer reds and yellows create a nervousness and seem to express anger or excitement. Harsh color contrasts generate stress.

These faces copy self-portraits by three German Expressionists, Max Beckmann (1884–1950), Ernst Ludwig Kirchner (1880–1938), and Otto Mueller (1874–1930). The colors of the original paintings are strong enough and unusual enough in combination to give the viewer a sense of unease. Consider the expression of each face, then color each in a way which supports that expression. Explain your color choices on the back of this sheet.

                   Studio Projects in Art History

Project 97: Expressive Composition

Composition can support a picture's expression. In his paintings Max Beckmann (1884–1950) struck at the negative features of society, the hypocrisy and injustices of twentieth-century life. He often squeezed grotesque figures of clashing colors into narrow, vertical frames. Such a confining composition produces a tension which underscores the uneasiness of Beckmann's themes. Compose a picture in this frame based on one of the following subjects. Underline the chosen theme.

The Injustice of Bigotry

The Shallowness of Materialism

The Despair of Poverty

The Terror of Violent Crime

The Corruption of Dishonesty

The Destruction of Drug Use

The Destruction of Alcoholism

The Horror of War

The Fear of Pollution

The Effects of Sickness

_____

other

Project 98: Depicting Feelings

Some of the paintings and prints of the Norwegian Expressionist Edvard Munch (1863–1944) directly expressed human feelings. *The Scream* and *The Kiss*, copied here, are two examples. Two other Munch titles are *Agony* and *Anxiety*. Read through the list of feelings below. Then depict that feeling in some way in the empty frame.

agony

anxiety

fear

timidity

sadness

boredom

despair

joy

excitement

anticipation

worry

terror

pride

disappointment

_____

other

Project 99: Street Scene

Expressionists frequently chose urban subjects in which stress, poverty, and injustice were most clearly felt. Ernst Ludwig Kirchner (1880–1938) and George Grosz (1893–1959) both did several pictures of German street scenes. The top drawing duplicates a detail from a Kirchner painting of a Berlin street in 1914. The preoccupation with fashion and city sophistication comes across as very shallow, especially on the eve of World War I. The other drawings copy Grosz's interpretation of the working poor of an industrial town.

In the empty frame, draw or describe a street scene which is typical of your community.

CHAPTER 27

Dada and Surrealism

As *emotion* is the key word of Expressionism and *construction* the key word of Cubism, *imagination* is the key word of Surrealism. Although the other movements certainly involve imagination, it is the complete release of the imagination which is the outstanding feature of Surrealism. The Dada movement can be seen as the forerunner of Surrealism in its imaginative approach, and it includes some artists who later created works in the surrealistic style.

There are two kinds of Surrealism. One employs a realist style, but jumbles the realistic objects of the painting, or combines them in confusing ways as it tries to create the impression of an unreal world with recognizable, realistically styled objects. De Chirico, Dali, and Magritte all worked in this manner.

The second kind of Surrealism is *automatism,* in which the artist seeks some way to unleash his or her unconscious mind, giving it free rein to create an image. Miró and Klee were such artists.

Because of the psychological basis of Surrealist theory, even the claim that its products come from the repressed mind, Surrealism has received much popular attention. Regardless of its theories, the fantasy of its creations, and public interest, Surrealism, like any art, must succeed with basic artistic ingredients: color, line, shape, and composition. Without the elements of art the imagination can be left with nothing. Therefore, the projects in this chapter stress exercising the imagination and using the basic elements of art in order to understand Surrealist art.

Significant artists:

Giorgio de Chirico, 1888–1978
Paul Klee, 1879–1940
Marc Chagall, 1887–1985
Joan Miró, 1893–1983
Marcel Duchamp, 1887–1968
René Magritte, 1898–1967
Salvador Dali, 1904–1989

France, Spain, Germany, and Switzerland

Dada and Surrealism
1917 and 1924

In the closing years of World War I several poets and artists, disillusioned by the horrors of war, organized a movement in Switzerland which they called *Dada*. Because art was part of the civilization which had made the war, they decided to protest with anti-art. They used junk to make art objects, composed collages from rubbish, and designed useless objects. Dada did not last many years, but it passed on its imaginative approach to the movement which followed, Surrealism.

The Surrealists believed they could turn the images of the unconscious mind into art, a theory which reflects the influence psychology has had on twentieth-century thinking. Surrealists often claimed to be painting the art of dreams as they unlocked the unconscious mind. Such a theory can be restated with one word, imagination, for it is imagination that produces the images of the mind. Paul Klee (1879–1940) created the dream plant, from which the illustration at right is copied, by giving his drawing hand the freedom to go wherever his imagination directed it.

Many artists called Surrealists were never part of the formal movement. Klee was not, nor was Giorgio de Chirico (1888–1978), nor Marc Chagall (1887–1985). Whether proclaimed Surrealists or not, all of these artists created art with richly imaginative images.

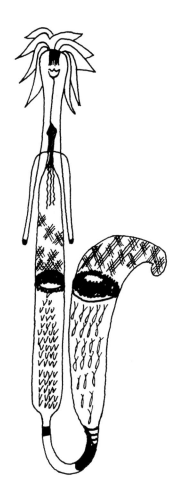

         Studio Projects in Art History

Project 100: Ready-made Dada

Some Dada artists took ordinary objects, altered them slightly, and called them "ready-made art." Marcel Duchamp (1887–1968) exhibited a bicycle wheel mounted on a stool, a perfume bottle, a snow shovel, and a public rest room urinal which he entitled *Fountain*. Man Ray (1890–1976) fixed tacks to the pressing surface of a flat-iron and titled it *Gift*, although it could no longer press clothes.

What ready-made object could you perhaps paint a fresh color, alter slightly, mount on wood, or frame as Dada art: pliers, a spark plug, or hair pins, perhaps? Describe or draw in the empty space your example of ready-made Dada art. Or, paste the picture of some object cut from a magazine in the space, draw any changes you wish, and give it a Dada title.

Project 101: Surrealist Creatures

On this page are gathered a number of creatures invented in the imaginations of several artists associated with Surrealism. They could only come from the imagination, not the real world. Create your own Surrealistic creature in the empty space to join those of Paul Klee (1879–1940), Joan Miró (1893–1983) and Marc Chagall (1887–1985).

Project 102: Surrealist Dreams

Many Surrealists created paintings which appeared as unreal as dreams. Yet they used conscious devices to present a disturbing picture, such as Giorgio de Chirico's (1888–1978) *Melancholy and Mystery of a Street.* Such devices are unrelated objects (empty van, small girl, dark colonnades), unreal space (steep perspective with several vanishing points), unreal atmosphere (sharp-edged shadows as if moonlit), and mystery (shadow of unseen figure and dark, empty colonnades). Use similar devices to create a Surrealist dream in the empty frame.

Project 103: Frottage and Automatism

Some Surrealists used special techniques to stimulate their subconscious minds to create visual images. One was *frottage*, another was *automatism*. Try one or the other in the empty space below.

Frottage: Lay the paper on a rough floor or some other roughly textured surface. Rub the paper with a stick of charcoal, soft pencil, or crayon. Develop a picture from the rubbing — a landscape, cityscape, science-fiction image, or whatever your imagination sees.

Automatism: Simply begin to move your pencil or pen in the empty space. Let one drawn line lead to another, as in doodling. As your imagination begins to see an image in your aimless doodling, develop it, adding facial features, vegetation, or whatever is necessary to produce an "automatic" picture.

CHAPTER 28

Abstract Expressionism

From the end of World War II until the 1960s, Abstract Expressionism dominated art. Because its principal galleries and the artists exhibiting in them were located in New York, it was first called the New York school of painting. Just as the United States dominated war-torn Europe in those years, New York was the art capital of the world. As the world recovered from the war, Abstract Expressionism became an international art movement.

Abstract Expressionism is an attitude as much as a painting style. Painter William Baziotes explained it when he said, "Whereas certain people start with a recollection of an experience and paint that experience, to us the act of doing it becomes the experience." The traditional artist first sees something or has an idea and then paints it, perhaps as a portrait or landscape. Mondrian carefully considered his abstract compositions before painting them. The Abstract Expressionist begins with no preconceived notion. The complete experience is the painting itself. Many Abstract Expressionists like Jackson Pollock came to it out of the automatism of Surrealist art, described in the previous chapter, letting the unconscious mind direct the painting process.

This is much more difficult than it sounds, for a painting with a subject has a beginning point — the subject itself. Students may feel inhibited and freeze when forced to create in non-objective images. The first project, "minute composition," can help to loosen them up. In another exercise students are asked to title three Abstract Expressionist compositions. It is not important that they find the proper title. The point of the exercise is to carefully consider abstract meaning. For the curious, the titles of the originals are: Kline, *untitled*, Motherwell, *The Voyage*, and Baziotes, *Pompeii.*

Significant artists:

Hans Hofmann, 1880–1966

Jackson Pollock, 1912–1956

Franz Kline, 1910–1962

Robert Motherwell, 1915–

Mark Tobey, 1890–1976

Helen Frankenthaler, 1928–

Mark Rothko, 1903–1970

William Baziotes, 1912–1963

Student Name _____   Date _____

Abstract Expressionism
1945

The Continental United States

In 1913 the Russian Expressionist Wassily Kandinsky (1866–1944) removed all recognizable objects from his paintings. His nonobjective art differed from that of other abstractionists who carefully painted and arranged colors and cleanly outlined geometric shapes. Kandinsky, on the other hand, let feelings lead him as he painted swirling colors and twisting lines. Because he was an Expressionist, his art was called Abstract Expressionism.

In the following years a number of artists practiced Abstract Expressionism, but it was only after World War II that it became a major movement. With Europe lying in ruins, the center of Western art shifted to New York City, where most Abstract Expressionists worked and sold their art.

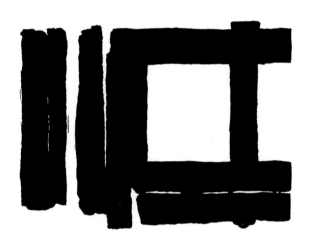

Painting No. 7,
by Franz Kline

The individual styles of Abstract Expressionism are as varied as a person's handwriting. Franz Kline (1910–1962) expressed a somber spirit with his heavy, broad strokes of black on white, such as the one copied here. His friend Jackson Pollock (1912–1956) dripped paint on large canvases, weaving webs of color lines as intricate as jazz music.

Jazz, because of its improvisational nature, influenced Abstract Expressionist artists who improvised as they painted. So did Zen Buddhism, practiced by some postwar artists. It instructs people to act spontaneously, and Abstract Expressionists did so as they worked. Beginning with no subject, Abstract Expressionist painting became a new experience for both artist and viewer.

Studio Projects in Art History

Project 104: Minute Composition

Select four different colors of felt pens, pencils, or crayons. When your teacher says "Go!" begin to color or doodle in the space below with one of your colors. Draw lines, swirls, shapes, whatever you want. When the timer says "Stop!" lay that color aside. With the second "Go!" begin coloring with the second pen or crayon until told to stop. You will also be timed for the final two colors. Keep in mind the arrangement of your colors as you work. Abstract Expressionists work much more slowly than this, but a timed exercise will help free you from any inhibitions of expressing yourself with color, shape, and line.

Project 105: Action Painting

The American Jackson Pollock (1912–1956) developed his own method of Abstract Expressionism which has been called "action painting." This is because when he painted he moved about, dripping paint from a brush on canvas laid flat on the floor. Sometimes he also dripped paint from a can with holes in the bottom. Now it is your turn.

1. Poke five holes in the bottom of a paper cup or plastic yogurt cup.
2. Hold it over the empty frame and dip a half-teaspoon of poster color into it, letting the color drip though the holes onto the paper. If too thick, add a bit of water.
3. As the color drips, move the cup around to get a variety in the lines.
4. Do the same for two more colors.
5. Complete your "action painting" by dripping color from a brush.

Project 106: Abstract-Expressionist Titles

The strictest definition of an abstract or nonobjective painting is that it contains no recognizable objects, only shapes, lines, and colors. However, the nature of those lines or shapes and their arrangement within a frame can express a feeling or an idea. These three drawings copy paintings by (1) Franz Kline (1910–1962), (2) Robert Motherwell (1915–   ), and (3) William Baziotes (1912–1963). Look carefully at each and give them titles, or select some of the following titles according to the feeling or idea you get from each drawing.

1 _____

To help you, here are some actual titles of Abstract Expressionist paintings: *Exuberance, Sacrifice, Cycle of Nature, Insects and Vegetal Forms, The Voyage, Shimmering Substance, Opposite Forms, Summer, Pompeii, Scent and Agony.*

2 _____

3 _____

186   *Studio Projects in Art History*

CHAPTER 29

Pop Art

Simply described, Pop Art creations sound as frivolous as they did when first presented to the public in the early 1960s. Bronzed beer cans, comic-strip enlargements, and pop-star faces done in an advertising style all seem as unartistic as they did several decades ago. Nevertheless, turning the commercial commonplace into art made Pop Art one of the most socially meaningful modern movements. For students it can be a great stimulus for their creative imagination. Pop Art subjects are familiar: the images of magazines, movies, advertisements, and television which students see every day, perhaps *too* often. How can such familiar subjects be turned into art?

The projects in this chapter suggest some methods, based on original Pop Art ideas. But students may well think of other ways to use advertising and the mass media. These are the objects of our daily life, regardless of what we think about them. Perhaps they cannot be turned into beautiful things, but by reworking them they do become something beyond themselves. At the very least, they become visual social comment on modern values. They can even become art.

> ### *Significant artists:*
>
> Roy Lichtenstein, 1923–
> Robert Rauschenburg, 1925–
> Andy Warhol, 1928–1987
> Claes Oldenburg, 1929–
> Jasper Johns, 1930–

Pop Art
1962

Abstract Expressionism made many Americans yearn for a return to realistic art. When it came, they were unprepared and once more dismayed. The new movement was called *Pop Art* because its artists took their subjects from the popular graphic art of magazine advertisements and consumer products.

The Continental United States

What was this art like? Roy Lichtenstein (1923–   ), a former window-display designer, created paintings which were enlargements of comic-strip pictures. Jasper Johns (1930–   ) bronzed beer cans and presented them as sculpture. Andy Warhol (1928–1987), an advertising and window-display artist, produced paintings of soup cans and Coca Cola bottles and made portraits of popular personalities such as Marilyn Monroe and Jacqueline Kennedy in a commercial art style. Robert Rauschenburg (1925–   ) made collage paintings which included photographs of current events: space shots, John Kennedy, and the Vietnam War.

The public reacted by saying such subjects were commercial art and not museum art. Pop artists replied that museums displayed seventeenth-century still lifes of wine bottles and fruit and vegetables. Soup and beer cans were their modern equivalent. Painters of royalty of centuries gone by would have chosen as subjects such pop queens as Marilyn Monroe and Jackie Kennedy. Pop artists created their art without comment. Yet, they were making a general satirical comment about their modern, consumer-oriented, advertising-inspired society. This is our culture, they seemed to say. Look at it.

       Studio Projects in Art History

Project 107: Superstar Portrait, Portrait, Portrait

Some of Andy Warhol's (1928–1987) Pop Art consisted of repeated small portraits of popular personalities such as Marilyn Monroe and Jacqueline Kennedy. The repetition suggests the repeated public exposure of such superstar faces, plus the eventual boredom we feel when their popularity fades.

Select a photograph of a contemporary superstar — a singer, athlete, television personality, or other famous person. Trace the face in a 1¼″ square, noting the areas of strong shadow. Use carbon paper to transfer the traced face into each of the squares below. When you have filled the squares, color in the shadow areas (in the way black has filled in the illustrated example). Use different colors, but keep in mind good color arrangement.

Project 108: Pop Art Supermarket

Some Pop artists turned food and household product containers such as soup cans and beer cans into art. They were saying that these are the things which are really important to most people and their labels are the art people most often see. Therefore, cans, boxes, and tubes tell more about the modern consumer culture than does any museum art. Select some kind of product container and turn it into art in one of these three ways.

1. Use the container itself as the art object. You might paint it with gold, silver, or bronze paint. You can mount it on a block of varnished wood. Give your art construction a title.

2. Make a design in the spirit of any twentieth-century art movement (Cubism, Expressionism, etc.) using your selected product container as the subject.

3. Some Pop Art sculptors enlarged consumer objects into plastic constructions. You can model your container subject in clay. When it has dried, paint it in strong, bright colors, following the design of the original label.

         Studio Projects in Art History

Project 109: Theme Collage

Pop Art collages differ from Cubist collages in that they frequently have a theme and are not merely visual arrangements of materials pasted to a panel. Pop artists constructed them from newspaper and magazine photographs, advertisement clippings, and even actual objects such as cloth and product labels, all in relation to their theme. Follow these steps to produce your theme collage.

1. First think of a theme which interests you (protecting the environment, human rights, gun control, etc.). Collect magazine and newspaper items related to the theme. Also pick actual objects (flowers, plastic forks, stamps, etc.).

2. Select the visually strongest items of your collection. Arrange them on the back of this sheet. They do not need to completely fill the space.

3. Using stick glue, paste each item in place. Paste only the corners or around the edges in order not to wrinkle the paper.

4. Add color to your completed collage with felt pens, crayons, or colored pencils in an Expressionist or Fauve manner.

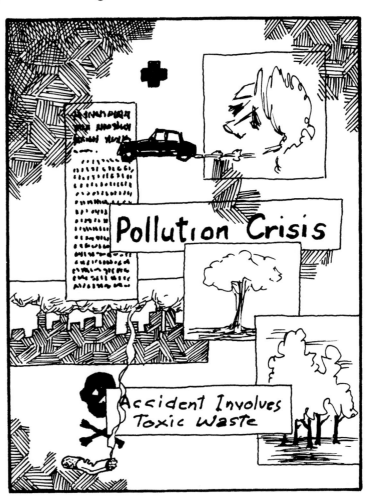

Project 110: Comic-Strip Collage

When Pop Art first appeared, people were outraged that its artists had turned commercial art into fine art. They were particularly upset when Roy Lichtenstein (1923–   ) enlarged comic-strip pictures into gallery paintings. However, Pop Art made people look more closely at popular art such as comics and magazine ads and discover their visual value. Now it's your turn to make art from comic strips.

1. Cut a number of panels from the comics page of the daily newspaper (no color).

2. Draw a ½″ border around the reverse side of this sheet.

3. Make a selection of the clipped comics panels and arrange them within the border. Don't arrange them according to their story sequence. Instead, make a visual arrangement. Denser, darker-toned panels must be arranged in relation to lighter, more openly drawn panels.

4. Once you have decided upon an arrangement, paste it in place with stick glue. Run glue just along the edges of each panel so the paper does not wrinkle.

5. When the comic-strip collage has been pasted in place, color it with colored pencils. Do not use the colors normally used in that strip; instead, choose and arrange colors in relation to the composition of the complete collage. Faces, for example, need not be flesh color but can be green, blue, or whatever seems visually correct.

Project 111: Enlarged Comic Strip

Find an interesting, colored comic-strip panel. Within the panel select a spot with a variety of lines and color and mark off a ¾″ square. Then enlarge the drawing within that square in the frame below. Include in your drawn enlargement not only the lines of the original but any fragment of writing that might appear and any printed dots that give color and tone to the picture. As you enlarge the detail in this frame, you can alter the composition somewhat to produce a more satisfactory design, but stick as closely as artistically possible to the original.

CHAPTER 30

Op Art

Op is from *optical,* "of the eye"; thus this is art that produces sensations for the eye. In a sense all painting is op art, for it employs color, flat shapes, and line to generate visual sensations. Perhaps the seventeenth-century realist art of Vermeer is the ultimate op art. But the Op Art of this chapter refers to the major art movement of the 1960s. Developing out of the earlier work of Mondrian, it was based on the painting of Josef Albers and Victor Vasarely. Built completely upon line, color, and shape, delivering no message, demonstrating no principle, it is art pure and simple.

Experimenting with color combinations means working in an Op Art manner. Therefore one project in this chapter borrows an Albers composition for student experiments. Students especially enjoy creating Op Art which teases the eye, the object of three of the projects. Reduced to visual tricks, Op Art is mere entertainment. But reduced to art's basic elements, to lines and colors, it is perhaps the most fundamental movement of this book.

> ### *Significant artists:*
>
> Josef Albers, 1888–1976
> Victor Vasarely, 1908–
> Frank Stella, 1936–
> Ellsworth Kelly, 1923–
> Bridget Riley, 1931–
> Richard Anuszkiewicz, 1930–

Op Art
1964

By the 1960s a new movement had returned art to nonobjective painting. This movement carefully arranged shapes and colors to produce a variety of optical sensations. It was called Op Art, a name sounding like the Pop Art which preceded it.

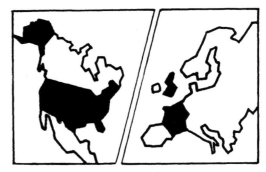

The Continental United States, England, and France

Op Art was related to earlier European nonobjective painting. World War II had brought Josef Albers (1888–1976), an instructor at Germany's famous *Bauhaus,* to teach color theory at Yale. His classes helped launch Op Art as a movement. Meanwhile, Victor Vasarely (1908–   ), a *Bauhaus* student, settled in Paris. There he explored ways in which color could produce illusions of movement.

The work of these two artists produced a difference between American and European Op Art. Americans explored simple, bold forms and bright color combinations. European interest was in visual effects, inspired by Vasarely's years of experimentation. European Op Art plays tricks with the eye. The English artist Bridget Riley (1931–   ) frequently used graph paper to plan elaborate designs which seem to vibrate or change character (notice how straight lines of this copied detail appear to curve). Some Op Art actually does move or shift colors, and so is called *kinetic art.* Regardless of approach, all Op Art is based on the fundamental elements of art, that is, color and form. That is true of all art.

Project 112: *Homage to the Square*

Pioneering Op artist Josef Albers (1888–1976) did over one hundred paintings entitled *Homage to the Square,* in which he explored color relationships. All were of the same design as illustrated here. They appear as a square of one color laid upon a pile of various colored squares. Using felt pens, colored pencils, or crayons, color each of the five empty diagrams. Think carefully about your color selections, then write on the back of this sheet your conclusions about each.

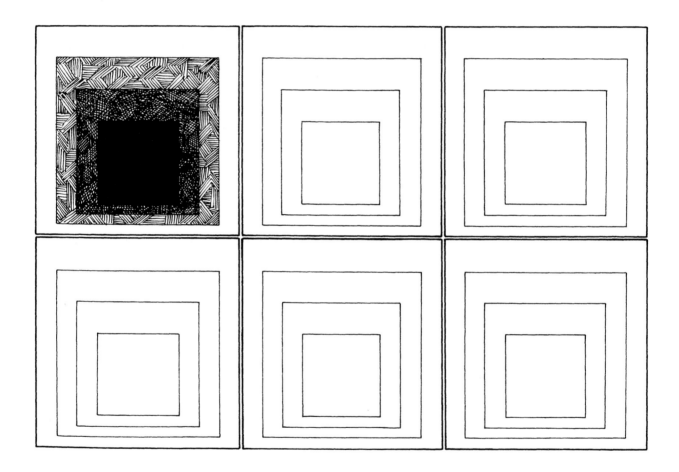

Project 113: Op Art Grid

An Op Art design can be automatically produced on a grid of rectangles of progressively varying sizes, as in this example. Use it or devise your own Op grid on the back of this sheet, then produce a design using the following steps.

1. Decide on a simple line motif: a diagonal line, a cross connecting each corner, a diagonal between every two rectangles, or something similar.

2. Repeat that motif in each of the rectangles of the grid.

3. If you want to make a color Op design, decide on some color scheme, such as adjacent spaces colored in contrasting colors, every four spaces the same color, or some other repeated color plan.

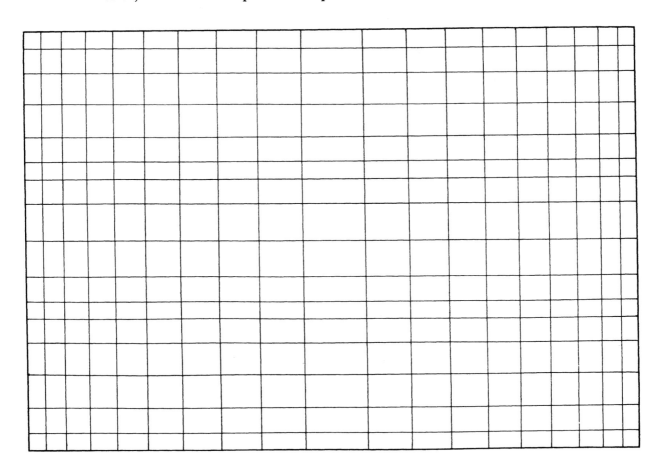

197   *Studio Projects in Art History*

Project 114: Op Art Illusions

Some Op artists have used optical illusions with which you might be familiar. Use the following explanations to help create your own Op Art.

Dimensional Effects: Lines drawn at an angle to a horizontal line give the appearance of three dimensions but can also seem to shift position.

1. Which is the front of the box, face *a* or *b*?

2. This is a rectangle sandwiched between two triangles. It also appears to be a ramp or a support for a wall shelf.

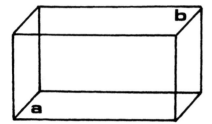

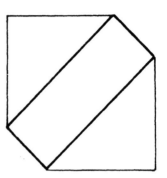

3. Do these doorways lead from the lower left to upper right or the opposite?

(continued)

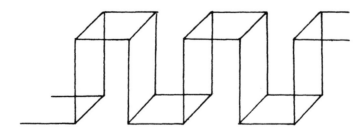

   Studio Projects in Art History

Student Name _____ Date _____

Project 114: Op Art Illusions *(continued)*

Afterimage: After staring at a strong color, you see its afterimage in another position.

4. You see gray spots where the white lines cross, the afterimage of the black squares.

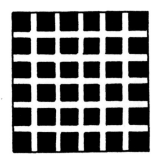

5. The afterimage of the white squares appears as gray spots where the black lines cross.

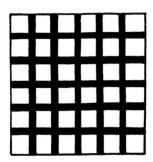

Contrasts: Interesting effects occur when contrasting shapes or colors interlock or are side by side.

6. The angled lines make the parallel horizontal lines seem to bend.

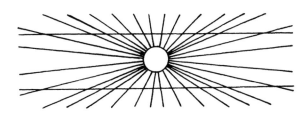

7. The contrasting black and white lines seem to flutter. Contrasting colors would as well.

Draw a frame 6″ square on the back of this sheet. In it create an Op Art design using one or more of these optical effects.

                                       Studio Projects in Art History

Project 115: Kinetic Art

With this sheet you can make a kinetic Op Art picture. When it is hung, the colors will appear to change as you walk past it. The color choices are up to you. Select carefully.

1. Choose three colors. Color all the zero (0) stripes one color. Color all the one (1) stripes a second color. Color the empty stripes with the third color.

2. Cut out the piece on the heavy outline.

3. Fold on the thin lines, as shown, so the figured stripes (0 and 1) are the sides and the unfigured stripes are the tops and bottoms.

4. Paste to a cardboard backing and hang as Op Art.

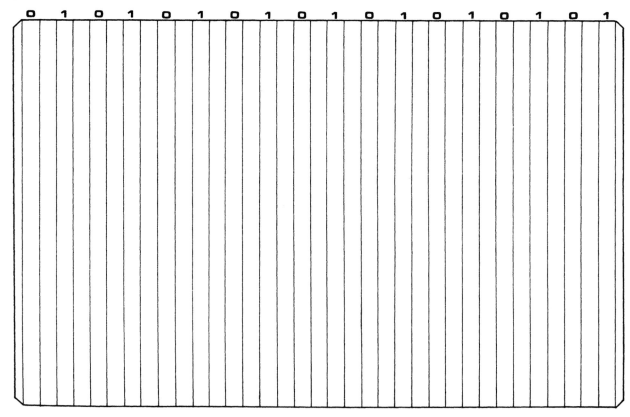

Glossary

action painting — A technique of Abstract Expressionism in which paint is applied through free movement.

buttress — Wall support on a building exterior. A *flying buttress* stands away from the exterior wall to which it is connected by an arch.

capital — The top part of a column, usually decorated.

cartoon — Originally, the preliminary drawing for a painting.

classic — Greek art of the fifth and fourth centuries B.C., or any art inspired by it.

collage — Twentieth-century technique in which various materials are pasted on a flat surface for an abstract composition.

column — Vertical post support of a building.

composition — In general, an art work. Specifically, the arrangement of objects, colors, and shapes in a work of art.

cool colors — Blues, bluish greens, and bluish violets.

cuneiform — Mesopotamian writing characters of wedge-shaped marks carved in stone or clay.

diptych — Two hinged leaves of wood or ivory on which a picture, usually religious, is painted or carved.

egg tempera — Medieval and Early Renaissance painting material with pigments held in an egg-yolk solution.

engraving — Metal plate into which a linear picture has been cut; a print made from that plate.

etching — Metal plate into which a linear design has been eaten by acid; a print made from that plate.

fresco — A painting rendered on fresh, damp plaster so colors are absorbed by the plaster.

gargoyle — A rainwater spout in medieval architecture, usually carved into the form of a grotesque creature.

genre — Art in which the subject is ordinary people in everyday activities.

gesso — Plaster-and-glue coating for preparing wood panels for painting.

gouache — Opaque watercolor.

hieroglyphs (hieroglyphics) — Picture-word writing system used by the ancient Egyptians and other cultures, such as the Mayan.

icon — Painted image of a religious figure; especially common in Byzantine and Eastern Orthodox churches.

iconoclastic — Literally, breaking of images; refers to the century-long period (eighth and ninth centuries) when icon painting was prohibited in the Byzantine Empire.

iconostasis — Screen on which icons are hung that separates the congregation from the altar in Orthodox churches.

illumination — Medieval manuscript page decorated with gold, silver, or bright colors.

lithograph — An image, drawn on stone with a greasy crayon, which can be printed on paper.

medium — The liquid in which color powders are held, such as oil, water, egg solution. Also the material through which an artist expresses himself or herself: watercolor, stone, oils, etc.

mosaic — A picture or design produced by piecing together small bits of stone, tile, or glass.

oil glaze — Earliest (fifteenth century) technique of oil painting.

pastel — Powdered color pressed into sticks (like chalk); pictures made from pastel sticks.

perspective — Systems for giving the illusion of three-dimensional space on a two-dimensional surface.

primary colors — Red, yellow, blue.

reliquary — Small, decorated container for holding some sacred relic.

retable (retablo) — Decorative screen behind a church altar, usually containing paintings and/or sculpture.

rose window — Circular stained-glass window in a church facade.

secondary colors — Green, orange, purple, the equal mixtures of two primary colors.

style — Similar visual characteristics which unite the work of a group of artists.

symbol — An object used in art which signifies a particular meaning.

tesserae — The small pieces of tile or glass used in mosaics.

tondo — A circular painting or relief sculpture.

tracery — The decorative stonework which frames windows and other openings in Gothic buildings.

triptych — Three-leafed altarpiece, with the two wings half the size of the central leaf, decorated with paintings and wood carvings.

warm colors — Reds, oranges, and yellows.

woodcut — A design cut into a block of wood from which prints can be made from the raised, uncut portion; a print made from such a block.

ziggurat — A tower, ascended by ramps, in Mesopotamia.

Project List by Subject

This list groups the book's projects by subject. Out of historical context, they can be used as general art exercises.

Color, light, and shade: 12: Color a Kore; 22: Book of Kells; 42: Shading for Solidity; 48: The Unfinished *St. Jerome*; 58: La Tour's Light; 63: Landscape Aerial Perspective; 88: Matisse and Color; 93: Mondrian's Colors; 96: Color Expression; 112: *Homage to the Square.*

Composition: 14: Athletic Prize Vase; 43: Linear Perspective; 44: Foreshortened Figures; 45: Renaissance Triangle; 46: Renaissance Tondo; 61: Dutch Still Life; 62: Still-life Collage; 78: Arranging Whistler's Mother; 82: Cézanne Still Life; 87: Harmonious Forms; 90: Cubist Composition; 94: Suprematist Composition; 97: Expressive Composition.

Design: 7: Egyptian Temple Columns; 9: Minoan Bull Fresco; 17: Pompeii Wall Paintings; 33: Illuminated Manuscript Letter; 34: Book of Hours; 57: Baroque Ceiling Fresco; 85: Toulouse-Lautrec Poster; 86: Art Nouveau Design; 92: To Abstraction; 113: Op Art Grid.

Technique: 2: Prehistoric Painting; 16: Encaustic Panel Painting; 18 and 19: Paper Roman Mosaic; 23 and 24: Egg-Tempera Icon Painting; 25: Miniature Mosaic; 36 and 37: Oil-Glaze Technique; 40: Simple Woodcut Print; 47: Fresco Cartoon; 79: Impressionist Technique; 81: Pointillist Technique; 89: Matisse Cut-outs; 91: Cubist Collage; 103: Frottage and Automatism; 104: Minute Composition; 105: Action Painting.

Subjects for drawing: 3: Mesopotamian Monsters; 41: The Art of Bosch; 52: Dürer's Religious Prints; 53: Holbein's *Dance of Death*, 54: Bruegel's *Land of Plenty*, 55: Rubens' Workshop; 56: Facial Expressions; 59: Genre Art; 60: Self-Portrait; 64: Rococo Pleasure; 65: English Portrait Painting; 66: Hogarth's Satire; 67: History Painting; 68: Antique Ruin; 70: Literature and Art; 71: Goya's *Los Caprichos;* 72: Blake's Illustrated Poetry; 73: Romantic Landscape; 74: Work Subjects; 75: Daumier's Faces: 80: Degas' Dancers; 83: Gauguin's Paradise; 84: Van Gogh's Letters; 95: Expressive Lines; 98: Depicting Feelings; 99: Street Scene; 101: Surrealist Creatures; 102: Surrealist Dreams; 107: Superstar Portrait; 111: Enlarged Comic Strip; 114: Op Art Illusions.

(continued)

Objects to make: 1: Carved Head; 4: Cylinder Seal; 5: Sumerian Shell Inlay; 10: Mycenaean Gold Portraits; 15: Roman Wax Portrait; 21: Early Christian Diptych; 27: Gothic Gargoyle; 28: Stained-Glass Window; 29: Door Hardware; 30: Decorated Reliquary Box; 31: The Bayeux Tapestry; 32: Medieval Tapestry Collage; 35: Decorated Book Cover; 38: Diptychs and Triptychs; 39: Gothic Retable; 50: Leonardo's Wing Machine; 51: Leonardo's Inventions; 69: Philadelphia's Roman Arch; 77: Victorian Photo Frame; 100: Ready-made Dada; 108: Pop Art Supermarket; 109: Theme Collage; 110: Comic-Strip Collage; 115: Kinetic Art.

Study sheets: 6: Egyptian Figure Proportions; 8: Egyptian Hieroglyphs; 11: Greek Architecture; 13: Greek Contrapposto Figure; 20: Christian Symbolism; 26: Gothic Architecture; 49: From Leonardo's Notes; 106: Abstract-Expressionist Titles.

Index of Artists

This index includes all the artists mentioned on the reproducible pages. It does not include the artist lists on the teacher notes. The italicized numbers refer to the chapter number of the student introduction sheet. The others refer to the project number.

List of Credits

This is a list of the locations of the original works used as the book's copied examples. Prints and works in private collections are not listed. Examples from the introductory reproducible pages are listed by chapter number, the rest by project number.

Chapter 1.   Top figure, Moravian Museum, Brno, Czechoslovakia; bottom figure, Altamira, Spain.

Project 1. *National Geographic*, October 1988
Project 2. Font-de-Gaume, France

Chapter 2.   British Museum, London

Project 5. British Museum, London

Chapter 3.   State Museums, Berlin

Chapter 4.   National Museum, Athens

Project 9 . Archeological Museum, Crete
Project 10. National Museum, Athens

Chapter 5:   Left figure, Metropolitan Museum of Art, New York; right figure, National Museum, Naples

Project 12. Acropolis Museum, Athens
Project 13. National Museum, Naples

Chapter 6:   Capitoline Museum, Rome

Project 16. British Museum, London
Project 18. National Museum, Naples
Project 19. National Museum, Naples

Chapter 7:   Vatican Museum

Project 21. British Museum, London
Project 22. Trinity College, Dublin
Project 24. Hermitage, Leningrad
Project 25. State Museums, Berlin
Project 28. Chartres Cathedral, France

Chapter 20. The Louvre, Paris

Chapter 21. State Picture Gallery, Dresden (destroyed 1945)

          Project 76. Lady Lever Gallery, Port Sunlight, England

Chapter 22. Musée Marmottan, Paris

          Project 78. The Louvre, Paris
          Project 79. The Louvre, Paris
          Project 81. Art Institute, Chicago
          Project 82. National Gallery, Washington
          Project 83. Art Museum, Basel

Chapter 24. Pushkin Museum, Moscow

          Project 89. Chapel of the Dominicans, Vence, France
          Project 95. State Galleries, Munich
          Project 96. State Galleries, Stuttgart, Munich

Chapter 28. Guggenheim Museum, New York